Cover image © Shutterstock, Inc.
Photo images throughout book © Shutterstock.com

Kendall Hunt
publishing company

www.kendallhunt.com
Send all inquiries to:
4050 Westmark Drive
Dubuque, IA 52004-1840

Copyright © 2012, 2014, 2018 by William T. Hoston

ISBN 978-1-5249-5883-1

Kendall Hunt Publishing Company has the exclusive rights to reproduce this work,
to prepare derivative works from this work, to publicly distribute this work,
to publicly perform this work and to publicly display this work.

All rights reserved. No part of this publication may be reproduced,
stored in a retrieval system, or transmitted, in any form or by any
means, electronic, mechanical, photocopying, recording, or otherwise,
without the prior written permission of the copyright owner.

Published in the United States of America

DEDICATION

To My Godmother

I dedicate this book to my Godmother, Thelma C. Owens, of Americus, Georgia. A former school principal and teacher, she has spent her entire life educating young people, mentoring them, and raising many as her own. I am also a product of her loving spirit. One of my Godmother's favorite gospel songs is, I Won't Complain. *Some of the lyrics state, "All of my good days/ Outweigh my bad days/ I won't complain." This has been the axiom of her life. Watching my Godmother, I have learned to H.O.P.E.: H.ave O.nly P.ositive E.xpectations for my life.*

To My Godfather

Andrew "Sonny" Owens

The only father I have ever known.

I've been knocking on God's door since birth/ My biological father didn't want me/ I prayed to the Holy Father, and He gave me a Godfather/ To witness my testimony/ Thank you, Daddy

To My Son

William Terrell Hoston Jr.
You were birthed to fulfill God's purpose for you
and take unconditional care of your mother.
You have the greatest mother in the world.
Daddy loves you.

Dear William Jr., you are the mirror of my life/ The reflection of everything good/ The disdain of everything bad/ My life has been good, bad, and ugly/ But you are the beauty from within that struggle/ Born to carry the torch/ And pass along to future generations/ Please do the world good/ For it deserves your service/ God bless you, son/ I love you

~Ode to W.T.H. Jr.

To My Brothers

Feddrick M. Hoston

Release Date: 01/20/2031

Cleveland R. Wilborn

Release Date: 12/21/2019

To My Uncles

Willie A. Holmes

Release Date: 05/14/2020

Recardo J. Holmes

Release Date: Life in Prison

Timothy C. Holmes

Released: 09/16/2013

CONTENTS

Acknowledgments ix

Preface xi

CHAPTER ONE
God Has Plans for Me, Bigger than I Ever Imagined 1

CHAPTER TWO
If You Embrace Negativity, It Will Hold You Forever 25

CHAPTER THREE
From a 1.9 G.P.A. to a Ph.D. 43

CHAPTER FOUR
The Road Less Traveled Can Lead to Success 65

CHAPTER FIVE
Being Content Opens the Door for Failure 91

CHAPTER SIX
Living a Significant Life 107

Motivational Worksheets 115

About the Author 145

Index 151

ACKNOWLEDGMENTS

My thanks, again, begins with God, family, and friends. All praise to my Lord and Savior, Jesus Christ. With Him, all things are possible. He has provided me with the four most influential women in my life: Mildred Hoston, Bertha-Mae Mitchell, Thelma C. Owens, and Janet Smith. I am a product of their hard work and sacrifice. In the words of Abraham Lincoln, "All that I am, or hope to be, I owe to my angel mother[s]."

To my beautiful and darling mother, Janet Smith, your examples of faith, courage, and sacrifice gave me much inspiration over the years to follow my dreams.

I want to thank my lovely wife and best friend, Cecilia Hoston. I love you. You have given my life such love, happiness, and joy. My wife and my son, William T. Hoston Jr., are my world. I want to thank them for giving my life more balance and purpose. To my son, Daddy loves you. "You keep me smiling / The things you do for me / *I Wanna Thank You*."

Thank you to Drs. Peter Anderson, Ralph Thayer, and Dr. Butler who provided sound advice during my undergraduate years.

Thank you to Kendall Hunt Publishing Company for believing in this project and their continued support of the LTMN editions.

To all of my former students at Florida State University, Florida A&M University, North Carolina State University, Xavier University of Louisiana, Dillard University, Herzing College, University of New Orleans, Northwestern State University, Wichita State University, and the University of Houston – Clear Lake, I say, "Thank you."

To the following families: Hoston, Zanders, Owens, Cosby, Mitchell, Duffey, Hooper, Nelson, Veus, Cooper, Franklin, Stewart, Gaines,

Robinson, Gauthier, Anderson, Powell, Williams, Campbell, Thomas, Bolling, Hicks, Burrell, Green, Greenup, Hall, Isodore, Trufant, Laurant, Washington, Clements, Vance, Bonner, Sephus, Volley, Calice, Spivey, Wright, Long, Sanders, McQuarters, Baptiste, Davis, Barbre, Lee, Taylor, Carter, Garnett, Watson, Bennett, Swiner, Gabriel, Johnson, Rainey, Lain, Mauricio, and the whole, "132 Villary Street!" #229Americus #504ForLife. #Hwy23ToTheEndOfTheEarth. #DTR.

To you whom I have not named, please know that even though you are not named in this book, I deeply appreciate what you have contributed to my life. Your contributions have helped this "Black boy fly."

PREFACE

*E*very so often when I get on a packed elevator, the person standing next to the call-box will ask the crowd, "What floor are you going to?" I sometimes reply, "Press the button for Heaven." Immediately, all those in the elevator will either become extremely quiet, smirk in disbelief from the response, or laugh under their breath. I've been doing this exercise for years. I mainly do it because I like to see people's knee-jerk reactions to my comment. However, there have been times where I've done it because I simply wonder what if we could push a button and be delivered to Heaven (or at least our own interpretation of Heaven or spiritual paradise)? What if we could push a button and erase our past hardships? What if we could push a button and change our current circumstances? What if we could push a button to become successful? What option would you choose? The irony is that since I was a child, whenever I'd enter an elevator, I'd press every button. My mom use to get upset and ask me, "Why?" I would always respond, "I need to know what every floor looks like."

Being in an elevator and pressing each button to stop on every floor is very symbolic of life. We are in constant pursuit of the "American Dream." We've been told life is about "the pursuit of happiness." Everyone strives to "achieve success." But how do we define these concepts and phrases? Your dream may not be my dream. Success for one may differ for someone else. We often define success by how much one has attained, achieved, and accomplished. Starting on the first floor of the elevator and attempting to work our way to the top. Does this pursuit come with a cost? Surely, to reach the top floor, there must be hurdles, setbacks, and sometimes new beginnings.

In my life, these buttons have been pressed:

Floor #1: Being born into a single-parent household.
Floor #2: Growing up without a father.
Floor #3: Being molested as a child.
Floor #4: My mother being addicted to alcohol.
Floor #5: Inability to make sufficient scores on ACT/SAT.
Floor #6: Having to quit playing college football to take care of my mother.
Floor #7: Each of my biological brothers serving time in prison.
Floor #8: My Godbrother, Rodney Cosby, who was my first role model, being addicted to crack cocaine.
Floor #9: Receiving my Bachelor's degree.
Floor #10: My grandmother dying of Alzheimer's disease.
Floor #11: Receiving my Master's degree.
Floor #12: Experiencing racial discrimination in my Ph.D. program at Florida State University.
Floor #13: Being displaced by Hurricane Katrina.
Floor #14: Criticism from the "Haters," "Doubters," and "Nonbelievers."
Floor #15: Graduating with my Ph.D.
Floor #16: Becoming a college professor.
Floor #17: Traveling around the world, motivating and empowering students.
Floor #18: Writing books. My goal is to write a total of 20 books. In 2010, I set this personal goal. To date in 2018, I have authored or edited a total of 15 books.
Floor #19: Continuing to work hard. I am a work in progress.
Floor #20: Heaven.
Floor #21: Reincarnation.

The goal of the third edition of **Listen to Me Now, or Listen to Me Later: A Memoir of Academic Success for College Students** is the same as I intended in the previous editions, to provide college students with key strategies and methods for achieving academic success. This edition continues to give important advice to students on how to approach and handle trials and tribulations, gain self-awareness, and become an active learner. The book is told through the lens of my personal experiences and that of experiences with college students in my years of teaching. In this edition, I have expanded the book with welcomed strategies, advice, and suggestions from college administrators, professors, staff, and more motivational stories from college graduates. Lastly, this edition adds motivational worksheets for students to complete to work toward academic and career success.

The central themes of attitude, faith, determination, courage, and perseverance remain the foundation of the book. As with the previous editions, the utilization of the pointers in this book will help to propel a college student's passion, determination, and drive to excel in the academic arena and in future career endeavors. This edition of the book continues to be an essential read for students that need motivation to stay the path and complete their college education.

In Chapter 1, I discuss attitude. Attitude means a lot. Throughout a student's college experience they will realize that attitude, not ability, will determine their academic success. Chapter 2 describes my upbringing and family life. I attempt to be transparent about the dysfunctional nature of my family to show college students they can overcome tremendous odds to earn a college degree. Chapter 3 details my academic journey going from a 1.9 G.P.A. after my first semester in college to earning a Ph.D. It is a story of determination to show college students that hard work does pay off. Chapter 4 expresses the importance of courage. It provides courageous testimonies from former students to inspire and motivate others. Chapter 5 explains the significance of perseverance. It encourages students to strive for academic greatness and not mediocrity in their pursuit of academic and career success. Finally, Chapter 6 expounds the difference between "achieving success" and "living a significant life." It moves beyond the goals of academic and career success to challenge graduates to establish themselves as significant human beings by providing value to the lives of others.

Within the pages of **Listen to Me Now, or Listen to Me Later: A Memoir of Academic Success for College Students**, I want college students to read with a conviction to become a better student and prepare themselves for academic and career success. The purpose is for students to witness their own experiences in the stories told. Hopefully, students will find hope, inspiration, and motivation to stay the path and achieve success. In the words of legendary basketball coach, John Wooden, "Success is peace of mind which is a direct result of self-satisfaction in knowing you did your best to become the best that you are capable of becoming."

My personal motto has always been: I just want to be an example. Many have come before me, and hopefully, those that come after will be inspired by the example that I have set. I have made mistakes and failed. But, I stand as a testament of hard work and dedication. I had to be an overachiever so that all nonbelievers would understand my struggle, feel my pain, and know that I would do it all again to right-fully earn my place in his–story.

CHAPTER ONE
God Has Plans for Me, Bigger than I Ever Imagined

". . . And I Made Lemonade."
(Abbreviated Version)

Unconsciously I float within this stratosphere / Unable to gain a mindset / That would support the inequality of this life / But consciously sometimes I have hid under the table / Afraid to emerge / In fear that those that walk amongst us/ May squash my dreams

I can't stop the tears from falling / A white towel hangs within my pocket / To absorb and surrender / I often yell into my thoughts / Trying to figure out a plan / To stop the wounds from bleeding

I do not know my fortune / The fortune given and taken / Then occupied by a stranger / A small piece of paper / In a snail shaped baked cookie / Manifests the key to my happiness / I wish it would give me six numbers to change my life

The writing on the wall tells the story / Illustrating that white paint confuses / More than it amuses the mind / Big eyes read between the lines / Entrusting me to decode / The blue lines that hold this paper captured

Call me the son of the unknown hero / I sail on the ship of dreams / Carrying the torch for those who are unable / The world is my oyster / But at times I feel I am just a snail / Awaiting my immersion in salt

For I search for a handle on this moment / Wondering what the future holds / But she released me from her embrace / Because I carry his name, William Hoston / Even the Devil was an Angel once / From the womb we are no longer attached / She put me out of the cradle / I am just her son not her baby anymore

My arms are too short to box with God / So I stand toe to toe with Jesus / Demanding that he answers my questions / And after he slapped some sense into me / We both sat beneath the crucifix / And squeezed lemons together

Hoston (1998); *written after my grandmother, Mildred Hoston, passed away; youngest brother, Feddrick Hoston, was sentenced to five years in prison; my mother didn't attend my Masters graduation; and started facing problems of racial discrimination in my Ph.D. program at Florida State University.*

Attitude

I AM 100% RESPONSIBLE FOR MY ATTITUDE. THE PRECEDING statement should be the Holy Grail for every college student. A student's attitude can be the determinant for their academic success. If a student has ever been through trials and tribulations in their life, were a participant in a challenging situation, or have resigned to being an average student, then they know their attitude can be a deciding factor in their decision to persevere or give up.

The importance of attitude is vital. A student has to possess the right frame of mind to excel in college. A key element is to maintain a positive attitude. An old Chinese proverb suggests, "He who is not satisfied with himself will not grow." The internal meaning of this quote is simple: Having a positive attitude will lead to a stronger desire to achieve goals and become successful. Students must make a conscious, deliberate effort to be positive.

Have you ever met a person that you believed "had an attitude problem"? Whether it was a family member, friend, coworker, or spouse, they always had a negative attitude. Every time that particular person leaves your presence you say to yourself, "They have an attitude problem!" Their attitude is either negative or extremely critical, which makes it difficult for you to stomach being around them. In most cases, those with negative attitudes have good intentions; however, any decent motives they have usually get lost in translation from the negativity of their self-talk or body language.

How does a college student develop a negative attitude? That ranges from not liking a course to receiving a bad grade. Attitude, not ability, will determine a student's academic success while in college. A positive or negative attitude toward college can make a huge difference in achieving academic success. In the classroom, I challenge every student to have a positive attitude. I have a strong desire to either help maintain a student's positive attitude and alter a preexisting negative attitude that formed prior to the student enrolling in my course.

My personal belief is that it's not as important in life what happens to you but, rather, how you will respond to it. English poet and playwright, William Shakespeare, wrote, "There is nothing either good or bad, but thinking makes it so." A negative attitude can control a student's train of thought and lead to poor academic performance. Of course I recognize that life-changing and tragic events will and have happened in students' lives that led them to go through periods of negativity and bitterness, but in spite of this, they do not have to remain that way. College students need to develop behaviors and skills that lead to academic success.

Eric, a former student in my LSAT prep course at the University of Houston—Clear Lake (UHCL), was born premature. He was born at 23 weeks and weighed only 1.5 lbs. Doctors had given Eric a minimal chance at survival. His eyes were fused shut, lungs could not function independently, and he would require major heart surgery within two weeks of being born. After the surgery, he weighed a mere 14 ounces. The doctors administered an experimental drug called surfactant that, if successful, would separate the walls of his lungs enabling him to breathe. Doctors then performed three eye surgeries that would help to open his fused eyes. Eric was released from the hospital a little over four months later, which would have been his scheduled delivery date.

I write about Eric because, despite how tragic his life began, he persevered and never gave up. Rather than feeling sorry for himself, he maintained a positive attitude and worked hard to be successful. His circumstances gave him plenty of excuses to quit. Yet, he realized that quitting was not an option. His future aspirations are to become an attorney and work for the Department of Justice. Eric is a prime example of how maintaining a positive attitude can catapult a student over life's hurdles. He never put a limitation on what he could achieve because he knew that would ultimately limit what he would achieve.

Triumphant Eric

In May 2014, Eric completed his first year of law school at South Texas College of Law in Houston, Texas. After graduating from UHCL, Eric buckled down and committed to his LSAT studies. He took the LSAT twice. The second time making a score that would ensure acceptance to a wider pool of law schools. He was accepted to several law schools, however chose South Texas because of the supportive learning environment and the opportunity to be closer to family and friends.

Eric's advice to college students with similar goals is "to never give up. Never give in to any of your detractors or people that will hold you down. You have to believe in yourself in order to succeed. You have to find that internal drive in terms of why you continue to fight on and persevere."

T.H.E.M.

College students can gain motivation from a number of outlets—family, friends, mentors, role models, professors, listening to speakers, and watching motivational films. Once an individual has become motivated, how do they maintain it? This will be a constant theme throughout the book. Maintaining motivation in college is difficult for most students. For other students motivation comes naturally. As I've alluded, a positive attitude has the potential to keep the flame of motivation lit even during the worst of circumstances. A positive attitude propels a student to continue to focus on learning and making good grades.

On the other hand, a negative attitude shifts the focus solely on the circumstance that led to the feeling of inadequacy. Students begin complaining and not producing. Going to class, learning, and making good grades are not a top priority. Some participate in self-destructive behavior. Self-defeat is the worst defeat. The saddest thing for a professor to see is a student that wastes his or her talent. As the old adage goes, "Hard work beats talent every time when talent does not work hard."

When many college students experience failures, it lowers their expectations of themselves. These failures vary from making low grades to not getting accepted into academic programs. Students develop what I call "comforting attitudes," when they say, "what's the use?" "why bother?"

"I really don't care, I'd be happy with a C for the course." They resort to a mentality of mediocrity, not wanting to "try" harder. The once positive attitude they had about education has now become negative.

Students come to my office and give me what I call S.A.D. stories, S.eeking A.dvice D.esperately, and I give them H.E.L.P. advice, H.elp E.very L.iving P.erson. The goal is to give them constructive criticism. Yet, some students would rather be ruined by praise than saved by criticism. They form this "me against the world" mentality, or "us" versus "them" mindset, when it's really "them" against "themselves." Achieving success of any sort is an internal challenge. The "us" versus "T.H.E.M." mentality happens when a student's negative attitude leads to a lack of self-Triumph, self-Healing, self-Esteem, and self-Motivation.

Self-Triumph

The value of a college education is important. Intellectual icon Albert Einstein is noted for saying, "College is not the learning of many facts, but the training of the mind to think something that cannot be learned from textbooks." He also believed that, "Imagination is more important than knowledge. Knowledge is limited." According to Einstein, to become successful, you have to use your imagination in ways that have no boundaries. If college students use their imagination to believe they can achieve academic greatness, it is exceedingly possible that it will lead to a prosperous career path. Every student can achieve academic greatness. Every student can enjoy a prosperous career. And more importantly, every student can experience self-triumph.

Triumph is reached from a victory or major achievement at the end of hard work. In this case, self-triumph is reached when a student puts forth the hard work to graduate from college. Hard work is a decisive factor to achieving academic success. As legendary football coach Vince Lombardi was known for expressing to his players during practice, "The dictionary is the only place that success comes before work. Hard work is the price we must pay for success. I think you can accomplish anything if you're willing to pay the price." In order to experience self-triumph, a student must pay the price. *What is the career goal that you really want to achieve? How much hard work will it take to achieve it? What price are you willing to pay to achieve it?*

Every college student will define academic success differently. Most students will define success in the following ways: (1) For some students, academic success will be achieved by just graduating from college and obtaining a well-paying job. (2) Others wish to have a high G.P.A. during their undergraduate years in order to have the option of obtaining an advanced degree. (3) The rest will measure academic success by the number of degrees they have attained.

On the first day of class, I ask each student during introductions, "What is your name? What is your major? What would you like to ultimately do with your degree?" If they say, "English," "Education," "Sociology," "History," "Social Work," "Anthropology," "Psychology," or "Art," I usually say to myself, "They will need an advanced degree to be competitive in the job market." If they say, "Business," "Criminal Justice," or "Political Science," I also say to myself, "They will need an advanced degree to be competitive in the job market but will be able to find a reasonable job with an internship or some previous experience." If they say, "Engineering," "Math," "Computer Programming," "Physics," "Nursing," "Chemistry," "Occupational Therapy," I say to myself, "Cha-Ching!" I then explain to them the pros and cons of each major. The majority of the time I encourage students to seek an advance degree to become more attractive in the job market. Despite what their career aspirations may be, I always give them confidence to follow their dreams. Confucius says, "Choose a job you love, and you will never have to work a day in your life."

Self-Healing

When a college student is in pursuit of self-triumph, there is a great possibility that they will experience academic setbacks. Setbacks have happened to all of us. Whether a student had a grueling time completing a research paper and made a below average grade or bombed a test they had studied weeks for, students have to keep in mind that setbacks are temporary. They still can prevail in the worst of times. As American televangelist Robert H. Schuller is known for saying, "Tough times never last, but tough people do." Even in the most discouraging situations, students can improve. Students have to maintain a positive attitude and challenge themselves to improve. My grandmother used to always tell me, "The biggest room in the world is the room of improvement."

For instance, Angela, a sophomore student I taught years ago at Xavier University of Louisiana, aspired to go to pharmacy school. She cruised through high school, making straight A's, and graduated salutatorian. Her first academic challenge came while taking organic chemistry. She had a tough time passing the course and contemplated changing her major. Angela had already taken the course once and made a D. She was in organic chemistry for the second time hoping to improve her grade. When we talked about the situation, I was adamant that she remains in the course and try her best. "Professor Hoston, what if I make a poor grade again?" she asked with tears in her eyes. I replied, "Angela, instead of asking what if you perform poorly, you should ask what do I have to do to succeed in this course?" Her response was, "I've studied, gotten tutoring, and visited the professor's office to ask for help. I don't know what else to do." My advice was, "Angela, I want you to keep your attitude positive. I also want you to work harder and study longer. The more effort you put forth, the more competent you will become in your ability to excel academically. This will in turn build your self-esteem to perform well in this course."

Angela finished the course with a C. Initially, she was disappointed by the average grade. When she visited my office the following semester, I reinforced my previous advice. I told her to continue to work hard and keep her energy positive. Use this experience as motivation for improvement. She still had two years to raise her G.P.A. I ended our discussion with a quote from motivational speaker Anthony D'Angelo, "The only real failure in life is one not learned from." These days, Angela looks back on that period in her life and laughs. After making a C in organic chemistry, she worked to repair her G.P.A. and positioned herself for admittance to pharmacy school. Angela finished her undergraduate degree in chemistry with a 3.76 G.P.A.

Self-Esteem

American essayist and poet Ralph Waldo Emerson wrote, "To be yourself in a world that is constantly trying to make you something else is the greatest accomplishment." When students enter college in their freshman year there is a big adjustment, academically and socially. It is important for students to have a positive adjustment period and transition to college life. There is a lot to digest the first year in college—new environment, new friends, and new courses. It is very common for students to become homesick. However, students should give themselves time to adapt to the new surroundings. Incoming freshmen should attempt to forge a connection with roommates, attend class to set a routine, and involve themselves in student groups and organizations. This will help to establish a stable environment to achieve academic success. Without it, students are more likely to make poor grades and some will eventually drop out of school.

Regardless of what age a student enters college, many students experience the same transitional difficulties. For example, Tara was a 48-year-old incoming freshman that enrolled in my political science course at Wichita State University (WSU). After graduating from high school, she got married, had three children, and took a job working at the post office. Her oldest daughter had recently graduated from high school and decided to attend WSU. Tara also decided to enroll in college. She had always wanted to attend college but the rigors of having a family and raising children were too arduous. Now that one of her children had graduated and the other two were in high school, this was a perfect time to obtain her college degree.

On the first exam, Tara failed miserably. After the next class period, I asked her to come to my office and discuss her exam. She began to explain, "Dr. Hoston, this is all new to me. I haven't been in school in 20 years. I feel out of place. I am the oldest person in the class. I don't know any other students and I'm afraid to talk during discussion." Tara was intimidated by the fact she was an older student. She was beginning to believe that college was only for younger students. In turn, it lowered her self-esteem. I had to put in plain words that college is a place full of diversity, which includes students of all ages. To help build her self-esteem, I imparted to her a quote from British author George Eliot, "It is never too late to be what you might have been." I then went on to tell her a story about my adopted brother, Jeffery Duffey, who had returned to college after a 17-year hiatus and had similar feelings. I explained to her it was imperative to stay positive and finish college. It was essential for her children to see their mother obtain her Bachelors degree. She would be a great source of inspiration for them. Tara heeded my advice; she joined student clubs on campus and made new friends. She realized there were other older students on campus that had gone through the same adjustment period. Tara completed her degree in social work and today works as a guardian ad litem representing the interest of abused children.

Self-Motivation

All college students are capable of achieving their goals and dreams. Far too many college students do not believe, therefore they do not achieve. If this is their belief system, the outcome will always render the same results: *Mediocrity*. Mediocrity is a synonym for "average." I preach to my students not to be average. The world is filled with individuals that are content with being average. One of my favorite quotes is, "Being content opens the door for failure."

This quote came about one semester when teaching African-American politics at Northwestern State University (NSU). Before each class, I would read a quote and support it with a parable that explained its meaning. Some days I would read a quote and have students provide their own interpretation. This particular day I had each student formulate an inspirational quote to be used as motivation. Afterward, the students were asked to write their quote on the chalkboard. After each student wrote their quote and explained what it meant to them, some revised their quotes to truly capture its significance. One of my students, LaKeisha, had this final quote: "Being content opens the door for failure." This quote encapsulated her level of motivation perfectly.

I first met LaKeisha as a 17-year-old freshman. She was in my state and local government course. Class started at 8 a.m. In early courses, I go to class before students arrive and make sure the lights are on and projector is warmed up. When I entered the classroom at 7:30 a.m. on the first day she was already there reading her textbook. LaKeisha was bright-eyed, bushy tailed, and excited to learn. Her energy was exuberant—huge smile and very polite. I initially thought her demeanor was such because she was a freshman and it was the first day of class. I soon learned she was like that in every class. LaKeisha had a passion for learning and told me during introductions on the first day she wanted to become an attorney. When she told me, I believed her. Many freshman students tell professors they want to graduate from college and go on to receive an advanced degree. Few of them, during their college years, actually put forth the academic effort to accomplish this goal.

LaKeisha was from a small town in Louisiana. She was the first in her immediate family to go to college and graduate. Her father never attended college and mother started but did not finish. Her father raised LaKeisha in a single-parent household. He worked hard and made tremendous self-sacrifices to provide a good life for LaKeisha and her sister. Her father's efforts inspired LaKeisha to do well in school and graduate. She went on to receive her Bachelors degree and graduated from law school. The special thing about LaKeisha is not that she accomplished her dream of becoming an attorney but that she was motivated from the first day of her freshman year in college. She understood that dreams don't come looking for you, a student has to chase them. Her positive attitude led to positive results. When I pleaded to students not to be average, she always told me she wouldn't. When I explained to students that sometimes 100% effort is not good enough, she always told me she understood. When I challenged her to be the best student in the class, she presented exemplary work. When the voice of greatness called her, she was ready to answer. LaKeisha's motivation was a fire that burned from within. It was lit at an early age and continues to burn brightly to this day. She wasn't content with her past circumstances and used it to fuel her motivation. Ultimately, she realized that being content opens the door for failure.

Jubilant LaKeisha

At a young age, I made a daily declaration, "I'm going to be an attorney!" When I learned the positive impact that becoming an attorney could have on my community, it became my life's purpose. After receiving my Bachelors degree from NSU, I attended the Southern University Law Center (SULC) in Baton Rouge, Louisiana. At SULC, I was apart of the Student Bar association, the moot court team, and tutored first and second year law students. I finished law school in May 2011 and was privileged to graduate in the top five percent of my law school class. I took and passed the Louisiana State Bar Exam. On October 20, 2011, I became a Louisiana practiced attorney. My legal career started in Natchitoches, Louisiana. After three months,

I was afforded the opportunity to become an attorney who represents children who are in need of care.

Working with children in need of care inspired me to write a children's book titled, "Cankeyo: You Can Keep Your Dreams Alive." This book was written to inspire youth to dream and fulfill their God-given purpose. The story is about three young girls who became friends in grade school. All three had a God-given purpose to positively impact their community. The book is based on a true story. I've had the pleasure of reading the book to elementary students all over Northern Louisiana.

The one piece of advice I want to leave to college students is to write down your goals. This allows you to prioritize and strive to accomplish them. It is important to work your hardest to achieve all of them. So when you die, you can die empty, leaving no goals, no dreams, or visions unfulfilled. As the late, great Dr. Maya Angelou would say, "Don't make money your goal. Instead, pursue the things you love doing and then do them so well that people can't take their eyes off of you."

When students are finished, count the number of answers marked in the *A* column and enter that number in the tally below the *A*s. Repeat the same process for the *B* column. This will help to determine a college student's current level of motivation. Students that have a higher tally in the *A* column currently hold a higher level of motivation. Those with a higher tally in the *B* column need to work to improve their level of motivation. In sum, the motivation questionnaire is used to gather information to help college students increase their level of motivation.

Humble Yourself to the Situation and/or Experience

A critical piece of advice I frequently impart to college students is for them to humble themselves to the situation and/or experience. All too often, as human beings, we become engulfed in trivial differences with individuals that we perceive to be in the way of our success. What we must understand is that achieving the bigger goal is what is most important. For example, many college students enter my office and say, "Dr. Hoston, I believe my English professor, Dr. Doe, hates me!" I usually reply, "Why do you believe that the professor hates you?" That student will say, "S/he always finds something wrong with my papers, s/he gives me failing grades on all my assignments, or s/he never replies to my emails." The student will become discouraged and want to exert less effort in the class. This behavior will inevitably lead to a low grade when the goal is to make the best grade possible.

My advice to them is always to, "Humble yourself to the situation and/or experience and not the person." Also, I tell them to send the professor an email, schedule a meeting, and ask to review their materials in a polite manner. The majority of professors, especially at the undergraduate level, do not develop personal grudges against students. Professors just want to see students work hard, hand in assignments on time, and show effort on exams. The desire from the student to receive an A should be greater than concerning themselves with how they perceive a professor to feel about them personally. Put simply, they are the professor, you are the student, perform all tasks in the course to the best of your ability, receive the final grade, and move on. If there is a discrepancy, as stated earlier, send the professor another email, schedule a meeting, and ask to review your past assignments and exams in a polite manner. If the professor does not respond to the email, visit him or her during office hours and discuss the grade. More times than not, this will rectify most grievances a student may have.

Jamie is a good example of someone that humbled herself to the experience and not the person. She was an A student and graduating senior majoring in criminal justice with aspirations to pursue her Masters degree. Jamie approached me at the beginning of the spring semester and said, "Dr. Hoston I want to do an internship." After expressing that she was interested in working with female at-risk youth, I suggested a girl's group home. She then enrolled in my internship course. Quickly Jamie found a suitable internship match, applied, passed the background check and drug screening, and began the internship. Less than a month into the internship, one of the supervisors called and informed me that Jamie was unpleasant to work with and should not receive a passing grade for the course. Initially, I was shocked by the call because Jamie had been one of my most pleasant students, always polite, well mannered, and respectful of others. I informed the supervisor that I would have a talk with her. I emailed Jamie and set up an appointment to discuss this issue.

When Jamie arrived at my office I informed her of the supervisor's call. She was totally caught off guard by the accusations. Jamie told me that the supervisor who contacted me was relatively new and had only supervised her one time. In fact, she was doing such a good job at the internship that the director of the girl's home offered her a full-time position with benefits. The supervisor that called had become upset with the director taking a liking to Jamie and offering her a position. Jamie was furious upon hearing the news. "Dr. Hoston, I'm mad that someone would try to jeopardize this opportunity for me." My advice to Jamie was to keep a positive attitude and humble herself to the experience and not the person. I further made clear to Jamie that on her way to success she would have to deal with many individuals that would become displeased with her effort and hard work because it would also make them accountable for their actions. Keep conflicts impersonal. Fight the issue, not the person.

Jamie finished the internship. The director provided me with a glowing evaluation of Jamie's performance and she received an A in the course. She humbled herself to the situation and/or experience and it paid off.

Are "Failing Moments" the Key to Success?

Muhammad Ali, former heavyweight champion boxer, social activist, and international icon, once confessed, "I hated every minute of training, but I said, 'Don't quit. Suffer now and live the rest of your life as a champion.'" Ali won his first heavyweight championship at 22 years of age. He was involved in several historic boxing matches, twice losing title fights early in his boxing career. In spite of these failing moments, he kept a positive attitude and continued to work diligently to regain the boxing crown. Ali was the first boxer in history to win the heavyweight championship three times. Even with experiencing a few failing moments early in his career, he is considered among many boxing experts as the greatest boxer ever. His nickname is "The Greatest."

Many of us are like Muhammad Ali. We are fighting to achieve our goals and, at times, we experience failing moments. Ali made the decision to continue to work hard, plug away through the losses, and try again to achieve his goal of being heavyweight champion. He wasn't afraid to fail. "What keeps me going is goals," said Ali. Too often we do not make the all-important decision to continue to work toward our goals because of fear of failure. What we must realize is that not making a decision is making a decision. When we sit idle after a failing moment we have decided to allow that particular moment or act to conquer us.

I can recollect a huge decision I had to make when I first began teaching. That decision was, how tough did I want to be as a professor? Did I want to be the professor that never gave A's? Did I want to be the professor that didn't care if a student came to class late, handed assignments in on time, failed exams, nor had an interest in them beyond that particular course? Or, did I want to be the "easy" professor that made sure students did their work but gave extra credit to ensure all students received an A?

I began teaching at the collegiate level at the age of 23 at Florida State University. Because most of my students were close in age or older than me, how was I to find a comfortable balance? When I was an undergraduate student, I had grown tired of professors who lost the passion to educate. Jokingly to my friends I'd say that if I were ever a professor I'd want to have an impact on every student I taught. I would require them to come to class, participate in class discussion, and make exams that challenged students to be critical thinkers. Now, years later I was faced with the decision to decide how challenging I would be as a professor.

In the beginning there were some ups and downs. I made a number of mistakes in how I handled students and certain situations. Like Muhammad Ali, I wanted to be the greatest at what I did. I prepared for courses with a fanatical work ethic and brought an enthusiastic attitude into the classroom. Also essential, I wanted to project the type of demeanor that gained respect but was welcoming to students. Despite my approach, there were times when I felt as though I had failing moments during the semester when students didn't want to come to class on time, didn't complete assignment, or wouldn't perform well on exams. Because I was new to teaching, I had a microperspective on student performance. I didn't account for the fact that not all students show up for class on time (or even go in some cases), not all students complete assignments, and not all students study for exams. My expectations were lofty. I wanted all students in my class to excel at a high academic level.

After teaching for an entire academic year, my expectations remained lofty but I made some slight adjustments. My philosophy was that wanted to prepare students for life beyond college. They should approach college like a job. First, I made attendance mandatory. You can't miss work, so you shouldn't miss class. Second, I learned the name of every student in every class I taught. This made them more likely to come to class prepared. If you have a meeting at work you need to be prepared. Third, I stressed to them the importance of presenting assignments of the highest quality. It would be embarrassing to make a presentation at work and the material you present have typos, grammar errors, etc. Last, I challenged them to make the classroom an intellectual environment by participating in thought-provoking discussions. At work the employees with innovative ideas and suggestions often impress their employer and become successful.

At the end of the semester when reading through the teaching evaluations, I was bewildered by the comments. Some students wrote, "Mr. Hoston makes us come to class. We shouldn't have to go to class." Others mentioned, "Mr. Hoston expected me to participate in class discussion but I don't like to talk in class. And he expects assignments not to have spelling errors. Sorry my computer can't catch them all." Overall, my teaching evaluations were good; however, those few comments bothered me. In my opinion, each of these comments represented a failing moment. I made the decision to implement what I believed were changes to my teaching philosophy that would most benefit the students long-term success. The fight to educate students

NAME _____ DATE _____

Questions for Personal Growth

1. If you had to be who you are today for the rest of your life, would you be happy? If not, what new habits would you adopt to improve your self-being?

2. What is a goal that you really want to achieve? How much hard work will it take to achieve it? What are you willing to sacrifice to achieve it? Can you overcome failing moments?

3. Are you ready to experience self-triumph? Will you put forth the effort and hard work?

CHAPTER TWO
If You Embrace Negativity, It Will Hold You Forever

"Pain."

Only pain resides in the past
    It sleeps in the crevices of sorrow
    Awaken by constant reminders

Forgiven but not forgotten
    The pain lies dormant
    Until the wound is re-opened

The wound bleeds from the inside
    A broken heart takes an eternity to heal
    The scars are just too deep

I've cried a puddle of regrets
    Attempted to smile until something happened
    But my facial expressions confuse my heart

Pain has been my greatest ally
    It has shown me how to continue to have faith
    Because of God's unwavering love

Hoston (2006); *written after Hurricane Katrina.*

Faith

AMERICAN PROLIFIC AUTHOR JOSEPH CAMPBELL WROTE, "FIND A place inside where there's joy, and the joy will burn out the pain." When I first heard this quote, I believed that it described my family life perfectly. I was born into a dysfunctional family. For much of my life I thought it was normal. There was no father present in my life. He had five children with four different women. My mother had an estranged relationship with her own mother for almost 15 years. As a result, she also alienated us from the rest of the family including my uncles, aunts, and cousins. The emotional pain of her self-imposed alienation contributed to my mother drinking alcohol excessively. My oldest half-sister had three babies at a young age. My two younger half-brothers are now both in prison but the signs were always there. My oldest half-sister and half-brother, two years my junior, are also first cousins. This is the outcome of my father getting two sisters pregnant. These circumstances have weighed on me all my life. But, instead of adding up my problems, I learned to count

Without a Father

The only time my father ever visited me was in the mirror. I never had a picture of him in the house while growing up. As I got older, I began to slightly resemble him. That was the worse thing that could have ever happened. As I will discuss later, it played a role in driving a wedge between my mother and I.

My father was merely a figment of my imagination. I use to imagine what our lives, my mother and I, would be like if he were a part of it. Those thoughts diminished with age. Growing up without a father seemed like the norm; therefore, I believed my life was normal. I later realized it wasn't normal. There is nothing normal about a man that lives in quiet desperation and willing to go to the grave without showing love for his children. The Greek philosopher, Plato, on one my blessings. A wise saying is that, "You never know how strong you are until being strong is the only option." I was only strong because of my faith in a higher power.

Each semester, one or two students will ask during a class discussion, did any of my brothers and sisters graduate with a college degree? Or, do my parents have degrees? I'll reply, "Only my youngest sister attended college." At one point, I would intentionally change the subject out of embarrassment of the dysfunctional nature of my family. Eventually, I grew candid about my family situation because I believed some student in the class could benefit from hearing an abbreviated version of the circumstances I listed above. I tried to have faith over the years that my brothers and sisters would see me as an example and want to better themselves. This chapter was written out of necessity to show college students that you can overcome tremendous family situations to earn a degree. I hope that it is as motivational as the other chapters.

---

occasion said that, "We can easily forgive a child who is afraid of the dark; the real tragedy of life is when men are afraid of the light."

When my father was a child the Hoston family adopted him, Reverend Reed and Mildred Hoston. His name before being adopted was William Love, but there was nothing loving about him. Because he was adopted, I believed he should have understood the importance of being wanted and loved. It was difficult to comprehend how a man that was unwanted would not want his own children. Instead of becoming a responsible adult like my grandparents reared him, he wasn't a very good father and, as a result, it impacted some of his children that greatly needed his guidance. My younger brother, Cleveland, wrote in a letter from jail, "My life would be different if William had been there for me growing up. I blame him for a lot of things that have happened in my life."

Instead of hating my father, I learned over time to channel my energy. I used this circumstance to motivate myself. I had faith that if I worked hard something good would ultimately happen. Early on it was sports because that was a father–son activity. I worked tirelessly to become a good athlete thinking that it would impress my father. When he was supposed to come to my 8th grade football game, I scored three TDs, had 243 yards rushing on 13 carries. A few months later at my basketball game I had 32 points by the 3rd quarter. The 8th grade resonates with me because he only lived two hours away and in my opinion that was a short drive to make to see his son. After each game I would call him but he never picked up the phone. I then would call my grandmother and she always made excuses for him. Her love was so abundant. She just wanted me to continue to do well despite his absence.

In high school, he told me he'd come to my senior football game. When he wasn't there prior to senior introductions, I asked the event coordinator to go last to give him time to arrive. He didn't show during the ceremony but I was still confident that he'd come. I scored two TDs in the first half and each time ran to the sideline to see if he had arrived. He never came. He never called.

The pattern continued with academics. He arrived late to my high school graduation but never came to any of my college graduations—Bachelors, Masters, or Ph.D. The man that was merely a figment of my imagination was not even that anymore. I could have become angry, bitter, and filled with hate, but I didn't. I wanted to make sure not to use his absence as a crutch. When a child grows up without a father, someone must fill that void. As much as my mother and grandmother attempted to, it is difficult for a woman to teach a young man to become a man. My Godfather, Andrew "Sonny" Owens, and adopted brother, Jeffery "Fly" Duffey, eventually filled that void.

My Brothers

My greatest failure in life has been the inability to shape, mold, and influence the lives of my two younger brothers, Feddrick and Cleveland. They both allowed their circumstances to comprise the choices they made. Circumstances do not define you, but rather your choices in life define who you will become. Each brother endured his own set of circumstances growing up. I am a fond believer of the profound quote by American social reformer Frederick Douglass, "It is easier to build strong children than to repair broken men." Unfortunately, both of my brothers are broken. They needed to have a healthy and stable relationship with our father but he was absent. Each went down the wrong path in life and ended up in prison.

First, I will begin with my youngest brother, Feddrick. I was closest to him. My father was married to his mother thus when visiting my grandmother for the summer we spent time together. Feddrick was always excited to see his big brother. We talked on the phone and I sent him letters to let him know much I loved him. He is now serving a 25-year prison sentence for voluntary manslaughter and robbery. This is the second time Feddrick has been to prison. The first time he spent five years for aggravated assault and cruelty to children.

"My father was a good man. He really was. It hurts so much that he won't be here to see his grandchild grow up or be here to see me graduate," said Shanquilla speaking through her tears, the daughter of slain Eugene B. Clark. Mr. Clark was just 47 years of age when Feddrick killed him on January 21, 2006, around 3 a.m. in the morning. Shanquilla was his only child.[1]

My brother and his girlfriend were both charged with murdering and robbing Mr. Clark for $1,480 of his income tax return. Feddrick alleged that his girlfriend, 10 years older than him, convinced him to beat Mr. Clark because he attempted to rape her. From their physical confrontation, Mr. Clark suffered massive head trauma and a broken bone in his neck. The police report read that Feddrick was accused of "beating and choking" him "until dead."[2] Feddrick contends that he found out after he beat Mr. Clark and subsequently killed him that his girlfriend was lying about the attempted rape and only wanted to rob Mr. Clark of his income tax money that he was flaunting hours earlier at a nightclub.

---

[1] Michael J. Ross, "Hoston gets 25 years for robbery and manslaughter," *Americus Times-Recorder* (Americus, Georgia) January 10, 2008, pg. A1.
[2] *ibid*

On January 9, 2008, nearly two years after the incident, my brother plead guilty to voluntary manslaughter and robbery. Feddrick originally wanted to stand trial for the case, but soon realized his fate was sealed. He was sentenced to 25 years in prison, 20 years for voluntary manslaughter and 5 for robbery to be served consecutively. Later, in a separate trial, he testified against his ex-girlfriend and she was sentenced to life in prison.

In comparison, my middle brother Cleveland was born two years after me. My father and his mother never married nor were involved in a serious relationship. In fact, I did not learn about him until my sophomore year in high school. When we met, we automatically clicked. I made sure to call and write him as well. I wanted to establish a relationship with the brother I never knew.

Cleveland has a lengthy criminal record ranging from burglary, aggravated assault, to cocaine distribution. When we were younger, I remember talking to him on the phone and he said, "Bro, I'm about to drop out of high school and get this money. I need to bring some cash in the crib, we are struggling." I knew Cleveland was on the road most traveled by young black men that feel the need to have to contribute to their households when no father is present. He eventually began to hang with the wrong crowd. Cleveland developed a criminal lifestyle and that began the revolving door of going in and out of prison.

The actions of both Feddrick and Cleveland have haunted me for years. I often wished we had lived in the same state or even the same city. Maybe I could have influenced their choices and helped them overcome their circumstances. Ever since I've dedicated my life to educating college students and helping young people, it is troubling to me that I have been unable to affect them positively. I've talked to them repeatedly over the years—preaching, comforting, yelling, and cursing, but to no avail. We've had a lot of heart-to-heart conversations about turning their lives around. I love them. For that reason, I didn't judge them for what they had become but wanted to help them because I understood what they could be. Sadly, my conversations with them had no substantial impact.

Feddrick and Cleveland

I have been beating my head against a stonewall
Trying to make sense out of nonsense
But in nonsense there is strength

Could I have done more? And what I did was that enough?

I began to teach them the game of life
The game has rules they both refused to follow

Feddrick saw how I used to make my paper, but he chose to manufacture his own
25 years in prison for $1,480, that's a bad return on an even worse investment
A man is dead and two families are destroyed

Cleveland saw how I used to carry the rock, but he chose to slang it
When I was running through the line, he stayed in the pocket
Subsequently, the bad decisions of life sacked him

Could I have done more? And what I did was that enough?

We all came from 'him' and different 'hers'
Children of a fatherless generation
Numbers in a mathematical equation trying to find the answer with no proof
How do you tell a child he or she was born to be hurt?

I succeeded because of the numerator, my mother
She added, subtracted, multiplied and divided
Because she wanted to teach me to show my work to receive credit

Could I have done more? And what I did was that enough?

I've dedicated my entire life to helping young brothers
But I couldn't help my own

The Lawn Mower

When I was in the 5th grade my mother worked three jobs: (1) her full-time job for the U.S. Navy, (2) part-time job at K-Mart, and (3) part-time job at Dunkin' Donuts. She would go to her full-time job from 7:30 a.m. to 4:30 p.m. My mother would come home to make sure that I was doing my homework and had eaten, and then proceed to her first part-time job at K-Mart from 6 p.m. to 10 p.m. Afterward she would come home to make sure I was in bed, had my school clothes ready for the next day, and take a short nap. My mother would wake up at around 2:30 a.m. and go to her next part-time job at Dunkin' Donuts. She would call me at 6:15 a.m. to make sure I was up for school. Each morning when I answered the house phone she yelled, "Time to make the donuts!" That was a famous saying from a Dunkin' Donuts commercial. I would get ready for school. My mother always made sure she was home prior to me leaving. She gave me a hug, kiss, and each time said, "Have a good day. I love you. Them teachers better not call me."

The toll of working three jobs began to weigh on my mother. At night, I would often hear her venting on the phone with my grandmother Hoston about our financial situation and that my father needed to pay child support. Hearing my mother cry saddened me greatly.

During this time, we lived on the naval base in Glenview, Illinois. Every Saturday I'd go to the base housing center, borrow a lawn mower, and commence to go door-to-door asking folks if I could mow their lawns for a small fee. Afterward, I would hand the money over to my mother to help with bills. It wasn't much, but it brought a smile to her face knowing I wanted to help her.

On one particular Saturday, I started on my normal route. First, I went to my regulars, about eight in total, but on this day no one wanted their lawn mowed. Then I proceeded to a couple of new houses. Again, there was no luck. For me, no lawns to mow meant no money for the house, which meant watching my mother cry. This was a painful sight for me.

I waited about an hour and in a desperate attempt I backtracked, starting at the first house. I knocked on the door, "Sir, would you like your lawn mowed?" He replied, "No, I told you before I don't get paid until next week. Come back then." I left disappointed and went to the next house. Once more, I was told to come back next week around payday. In a stroke of genius for a 10-year-old, I began mowing their yards anyway. The patron of the home came out and asked, "What are you doing?" I answered, "Sir, I'm mowing your lawn. I need money to help my mother." He replied, "I told you I can't pay you today." I retorted with a phase I've heard my mother say many times, "Well, as long as you owe me, I'll never go broke." He walked back into the house and allowed me to continue. On that day, I must have mowed 12 or more lawns and only four people paid me. When I returned home, I handed my mother the money and again saw the smile on her face. I persevered through the rejection, actually being a nuisance to these individuals. However, I was determined to be the man of the house and help provide for my mother.

My Mother

The 16th president of the United States, Abraham Lincoln, once said, "All that I am, or hope to be, I owe to my angel mother." I love my mother, Janet Smith. She gave me life and I am forever thankful to her. My mother is from a small town, Americus, Georgia. She was the middle of nine children. My mother married, had me, and got divorced all by 21 years of age. By her own admission, she partly married my father because she was pregnant and wanted to move from the strict confines of my grandmother's house, Bertha Mae Mitchell. The marriage started off rocky and shortly after my father and mother split. Instead of moving back home, she went to Queens Far Rockaway, New York, where several of my uncles and aunts had moved. Soon after, I was born.

My mother joined the United States Navy (USN) when I was three years old. As a child, I traveled around the United States. Living in states such as New York, Georgia, South Carolina, Illinois, California, and a bunch of other places before eventually settling in Louisiana. She enlisted in the military to provide a better life for me than the one she had. My mother is definitely the foundation of my success. During the good times, she was loving, affectionate, funny, caring, giving, and an all-around good person. In contrast, the bad times showed that she could be mean, hurtful, and unforgiving. I speak of her in the past tense because, at the time of this writing, I haven't spoken to her in years.

I can remember as a child, my mother at times would become very upset with me. In her drunken, angered rage she would scream, "You are going to grow up and be like your father." That statement has stuck with me my entire life. In truth, it has been a source of motivation to strive to be better than the example that my father set. Although I know now that she did not say those words to be hurtful and malicious, they were said. And, they did have an impact. Throughout the years, I realized that her angry outbursts were driven by alcohol abuse. Most of the mean-spirited comments she directed toward me were made when she was drinking.

Her addiction to alcohol has driven a wedge in our relationship. My mother always enjoyed having a drink. Instead of keeping the liquor bottle at the bar or in the pantry, she kept it next to her bed. I always assumed she did it to prevent me from trying alcohol. It wasn't until high school that I began to understand the convenience of keeping the bottle near her. When she would first start drinking, we would joke, laugh, and have lots of fun. By the third or fourth drink, she became an angry drunk, irritated, and volatile. The same joke told an hour earlier that elicited a ton of laughs was now taken seriously. "Some times you make me sick, get away from me you remind me of your father," she would slur at a high octave. Her behavior was chaotic and unpredictable. Usually when she drank I would go to my room or if I had to interact with her it was like walking on eggshells. When she drank the likelihood of doing something wrong increased, which often led to a slap, extension cord beating, or punishment.

Late at night when I went to go to use the bathroom I would hear her crying and see her holding a drink. She was fighting the demons of her past and alcohol was the weapon of choice. There were many nights when I held her in my arms until she fell asleep. She was my mother, but at different times I was her father, brother, and best friend. My mother had an estranged relationship with her own mother and rarely spoke to her brothers and sisters. I told the two people that she did have a close relationship with, my grandmother Hoston and Godmother, but they didn't believe the severity of it until years later. My mother was a functional drunk. The only people that knew were the men she dated and myself.

Over the years, her drinking has gotten progressively worse. When I was in college she would call between 3 and 4 a.m. in a drunken stupor and tell me how much of a disappointment I had been in her life. Many times, she would put it in writing and send to me in the mail.

After my Ph.D. graduation I received a hand-written letter that said in one paragraph, "Having you was the worse thing I ever did." Although it hurt me to the core, I simply blamed it on the alcohol. Countless efforts to get her help have been denied. In fact, they fuel her drunken hatred toward me even more.

As I stated earlier, during the good times, she was loving, affectionate, funny, caring, giving, and an all-around good person. These will be the memories that I hold on to as she fights this disease.

The Next Time I See You

The next time I see you/ Your image will be different/ A far cry from how you used to look/ But the tears in my eyes won't let me see that/ The embrace will be familiar/ Like the day I was born

The next time I see you/ No apologies need to be uttered/ Both of our hearts are sorry/ I've prayed a thousand moments/ I've shed a thousand tears/ I've looked at your picture a thousand times/ And it said, "I love you," in a thousand ways

The next time I see you/ I want it to be on earth/ Seeing you in a casket would break my heart/ Please, please, please get help/ I can't live another day without you

Quality of Life Chart

In some courses, I give students a copy of the poem, *The Uses of Sorrow*, by American poet Mary Oliver. In the poem she describes how someone can leave darkness in your life and we later can use that negativity as a medium to gain a positive outlook. Often in life we carry sorrow given to us by others. Could this sorrow really be a gift? Could it be used for a greater good?

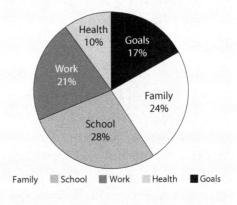

All college students will experience adversity. An unknown quote I like to use in class is, "Adversity causes some to break, but it causes others to break through." In class, I give students a motivational

assignment to make a pie chart of elements of their lives and we will discuss them. For example, the sections usually are family, school, work, health, goals, etc. Once students have divided the chart into sections that represent major areas of their lives, they then assign a percentage value and identify what areas need improvement. Most students normally begin each section in the 80 to 90 percentile range. The exercise is devised for students to gain self-accountability and denote what areas to work on. The assignment of percentages is purely random. The chart shows the sections from a freshman student I taught while at North Carolina State University (NCSU).

FAMILY: Her mother gave birth to her in prison. She then became a ward of the state going from foster home to foster home. In the 10th grade, her sixth foster home family adopted her. For family, she assigned 24%.

SCHOOL: She went to numerous elementary and middle schools, dropped out of high school at 17-years-old, got a GED, went to a community college for a semester, and was now a freshman at NCSU. For school, she assigned 28%.

WORK: She worked at the Crabtree Valley Mall in the food court. For work, she assigned 21%.

HEALTH: She was born with type 1 diabetes and had to carefully balance her insulin and watch what she ate. For health, she assigned 10%.

GOALS: She wanted to finish college, go on to medical school and receive her M.D. by 28 years old. For goals, she assigned 17%.

In the years that I had done the motivational assignment, I could not figure out how or why she assigned certain percentages to the sections. During the class discussion, she told us her major sections and percentage score but was very vague on why each section received the allotted percentage. After class, I asked her to stay behind. Her numbers were extremely low and I wanted to provide her with some words of encouragement. I asked her while erasing the chalkboard, "Explain to me why your percentages are so low?" "No need to worry Professor Hoston, I have it under control," she responded.

"Well, just explain it to me a little," I further inquired not trying to be too intrusive.

She began to put into plain words the plan for success. The 17% was assigned for goals because she received her GED at 17 years old. One of her old foster parents had told her she was too dumb to even get a GED. The 28% assigned for school referred to the age she projected herself to graduate from medical school. She wanted to graduate at 28-years-old. The 10% assigned for health reminded her that she almost died at 10 years old because one of her foster parents refused to buy her insulin. The 21% assigned for work was the age she wanted to start a non-for-profit organization that helped homeless teenagers. When she ran away from foster homes, she was homeless for weeks at a time. And last, the 24% assigned for family represented the age her mother was when she had her in prison.

Today, she is a doctor of internal medicine and also volunteers at local clinics helping at-risk teen girls. She realized her box full of darkness was a gift.

Are You Proud of Yourself?

Are your family and friends proud of you? Are you proud of yourself? A little secret that I have learned over the years is that you have to be proud of yourself. My father has never told me he was proud of me. I can count on one hand the number of times my mother has told me she was proud of me. Despite hearing limited or no verbal affirmation from my parents, I did receive it from my Grandmother Hoston, Godmother, teachers, and friends. Life has a funny way of balancing the scales.

Every time I speak to a crowd of students, especially a younger audience, at least one parent will approach me afterward and say, "I know your parents must be really proud of you." The statement is bizarre to me in a lot of ways because I honestly do not know. As I stated earlier, my father has never been to any of my college graduations. My mother attended my Bachelors but not the Masters or Ph.D. graduation. The only constant at any of my graduations from receiving my Bachelors degree to getting hooded for my Ph.D. were my Godparents, my nephew, Elgin Cosby, and two of my closest friends, Rolonda Clements-Martin and Kim Vance.

Throughout my life I just wanted to make my parents proud, especially my mother. She was ecstatic when I graduated with my Bachelors degree. I honestly had never seen her that happy. When I got accepted into graduate school at Florida State University (FSU) and was awarded a teaching assistantship, she was also overjoyed.

I have been teaching for nearly two decades. Unfortunately, my mother has never seen me teach. When teaching, I project my voice loudly in an attempt to keep students engaged and attentive to lecture. How that began came to me in a dream. When I first started teaching at FSU I was eager for my mother to come to one of my lectures. At the time, she lived in New Orleans, Louisiana, while I was in Tallahassee, Florida. It is a five-hour drive between the two cities. I used to constantly invite her to come visit me and stay until Tuesday because I taught on Mondays. I always had the feeling that she would just pop in and surprise me. In a dream I had one night, she came to visit me while teaching but couldn't find the classroom. Also, all of the classroom doors on that floor were shut so neither could she hear me. From that point on, I really started projecting my voice when I taught and I always left the door cracked. That way she could quietly sneak into the classroom, sit in the back, and watch her son. Many times when I'd finish teaching and walked out of the classroom there would always be a group of students (and sometimes professors) gathered in the hallway that said, "I've been out here the whole time listening to your lecture. I really enjoyed it. What class do you teach?" While answering them, I often scanned the hallway in hopes of seeing my mother.

Like I said, life has a funny way of balancing the scales. I recall speaking at a local church with two of my colleagues. We were holding a college admissions seminar for high school students, providing them with information on how to gain admission to college, fill out FASFA forms, obtain financial aid, and the rigors of freshman year in college. My part in the presentation was to close with a motivational speech. The small, personal setting of the church provoked me to communicate personal stories that I would reserve in a normal setting. After the speech, a woman approached me with her two sons, gave me a big hug, and said, "I pray that God allows my sons to grow up and be as blessed as you. You are the son that every mother dreams about having."

Questions for Personal Growth

1. Do you love yourself? If so, better yourself. How will you go about bettering yourself?

2. Are you proud of yourself? If not, what would it take for you to be proud of yourself?

3. What actions will you take to overcome negative circumstances?

CHAPTER THREE
From a 1.9 G.P.A. to a Ph.D.

Black Tax.
(Abbreviated Version)

The tax on the dollar, makes me wanna HOOLLLLLAAAAAA!
But I stay quiet, because my wage is minimum

For I sit at attention, in an upright position
Staring into your mind, weaving my way through your racist thoughts
Trying to grasp the knowledge, that exists in your left hemisphere

I'm a student of your intellect, couldn't trade me now for a jar of molasses
Even if I planted the seed in your backyard, and irrigated the land daily

My color inflates the economy, exemptions on my 1040
Makes you believe, that you should make this life hard for me

W2s give you the blues, it was once against the law
For Negros to read or write, from mis-education to education

Indebted to my ancestry, I gladly pay the price
The beginning of the alphabet, could never measure my struggle

Hoston (1998); *written after I received a failing grade (B−) in a graduate school course, criminological theory, at Florida State University, after having an A for the entire semester.*

Determination

"ATTACK THIS DAY WITH AN ENTHUSIASM UNKNOWN TO mankind!" I first heard this phrase while watching an ESPN football special on Jack Harbaugh, a longtime football coach. He'd often use it to motivate his sons, John and Jim Harbaugh. As the story goes, every morning Jack would drop his sons off at elementary school, place the car in park, lean back in his seat, and say to third grader John and first grader Jim, "Okay men, grab your lunchboxes." After the boys would gather their things, he would make eye contact and then say, "Now go out there and attack this day with an enthusiasm unknown to mankind!"

Jack Harbaugh was a football coach for a total of 42 years. In that time, he was a great motivator to his former coaches, players, and especially his sons. His oldest son, John Harbaugh, was a football player at Miami University (Ohio) and later worked his way up the college and professional coaching ranks to become an NFL head coach with the Baltimore Ravens. As well, his youngest son Jim Harbaugh, played football at the University of Michigan, was selected with the 26th pick in the first round of the 1987 NFL draft and played 15 years in the NFL. After retiring he also worked his way up the coaching ranks to become an NFL head coach with the San Francisco 49ers.

On one fall Thanksgiving evening the Baltimore Ravens and San Francisco 49ers football teams met in a clash of epic proportion. The media hype surrounding the game was how influential their father, Jack Harbaugh, was in his sons' lives and the joy he would receive watching them make history as the first brothers to coach against each other in an NFL game. Before the contest, Jack, John, Jim, and their mother, Jackie, met at midfield to take pictures of this historic moment. Jack and Jackie posed for pictures but left to watch the game in a remote area to avoid being a further distraction. When a female reporter stopped them on their way out of the stadium, she asked Jack what advice did he give his sons and he replied, "I told them to attack this day with an enthusiasm unknown to mankind!"

Determination will help a college student overcome the pitfalls of many "failing moments" as talked about in Chapter 1. Like Jack Harbaugh taught his children, it is central to the success of students to attack their day with an enthusiasm unknown to mankind. I entered college on a football scholarship at a small college, Nicholls State University (NSU). The National Collegiate Athletic Association (NCAA) refers to college students on athletic scholarship as student-athletes—be a student first and athlete second. My desire to attend college was not motivated by academics. I only wanted to play football—be an athlete first and student second. Hopefully, that would land me in the NFL and I could make enough money that my mother would never have to work another day in her life.

In my senior year of high school, I had a difficult time passing the standardized entrance test to qualify for a football scholarship. I took the ACT three times and SAT once. The first time I took the ACT I made a 13. The second time I scored a 15. The NCAA required a 17 on the ACT to qualify. Then I switched to the SAT and scored below the required 700 combined score. Universities and colleges that were interested in offering me a scholarship withdrew consideration. Many of them did not believe I could make a qualifying score. After the National Signing date had passed to sign football recruits, only two schools still had any interest, Nicholls State University and Northwestern State University, both in Louisiana.

The vice principal of my high school, Pat Duplessis, had been mentoring me throughout this process. Coach Pat, as many called him, was a respected mentor and father figure to countless students. He taught various sports as well as being an educator. When schools lost interest we put together a football highlight tape and an attached letter that explained how diligently I was working to make a score on either the ACT or SAT that would qualify me for a scholarship. In the midst of it all, Coach Pat said to me, "Son, have you considered that football may not be your path to success?" At 17-years-old, it was difficult for me to interpret the meaning behind his statement. "If you approached academics as you approach your training for athletics, you'd have an academic scholarship," he added. Those two statements went in one ear and out the other.

Before I left Coach Pat's office, I said, "Coach, I am determined to pass this test. I can't let it defeat me." He replied, "You've just made my point. All choices lead you somewhere." This was again, in one ear and out the other. I studied and studied and studied looking over ACT materials. When the day of the exam came I was slightly nervous. As I entered the testing center there was a quote on one of

1.9 G.P.A. Nicholls State University (NSU)

After my first semester in college I had a 1.929 G.P.A. I started with six courses and dropped one. They were remedial English, algebra 101, turf management, student success, history of Western civilization, and basketball. The semester began on task. Football players had breakfast check in the mornings to make sure we were up and ready for class. After breakfast, I then went to class, football practice, and ended the day at study hall. That soon changed as I was easily influenced by others not to go to class. Eventually after breakfast check I would hang out in the student union. Either I'd play cards, ping-pong, video games, or pool until football practice. Seldom did I go to class, only on exam days.

At the midterm, the athletic academic advisor received a report with our grades. In our one-on-one meeting, she began with a quote from American humorist, Arnold Glasow, "William, improvement begins with I." Prior to the meeting, I had developed 101 excuses for my low academic performance. The one that I was going to use was, "Ma'am, I'm having a hard time adjusting academically with going to class and playing football." Before I could speak a word, she started with the quote and reprimanded me for my awful grades.

There was no improvement the following semester. I took four courses and ended the semester with a 1.5 G.P.A. It started off on a the walls that read, "All choices lead you somewhere, bold choices take you where you are suppose to be." That was a celebratory day because I scored the needed 17 on the ACT to qualify for a football scholarship. More notably, I began to put into perspective that football was not the only gateway to success. The above-mentioned quote by American actor, Willem Dafoe, captures that moment of enlightenment when I realized that my determination to become successful could be achieved in other ways. I was only determined to pass the test to play football when I should have been determined to pass the test to be admitted to a respectable university or college. That would have been the bold choice.

---

good note. The goal was to study and work to improve my G.P.A. However, on Valentine's day after visiting my girlfriend, I received a call from my mother who was stationed in Pt. Mugu, California. When I picked up the phone, I could hear her crying on the other end. She began to explain why she was crying, circumstances that had arose, and that she wanted me to come to California while she was going through a difficult time in her life. From that point forward, neither school nor football was a priority. The only thing that mattered was going to California to check on my mother. A week before spring football was to start I informed the coaches of my decision. That was my last semester at Nicholls State University and playing football in college. The NFL dream had ended on a disappointing note.

Oxnard Community College (OCC)

In California, I attended Oxnard Community College. That was a pivotal time in my life. I only went for one semester but ended it with a 3.462 G.P.A. and a boatload of academic confidence. An important influence at OCC was Ms. Butler. She was my sociology instructor. The reason why Ms. Butler left a lasting impression was because of her blunt honesty and determination to get the best academic effort from me. Because I no longer had football as a motivator to excel in the classroom, I continued not to take my academic studies seriously. This was very similar to the pattern I developed in my second semester at NSU.

One day, we were given a presentation assignment to discuss our past, present, and future life course. The assignment was based on how our past has shaped us, how our future is molding us, and our goals for the future. When it was my time to present I gave a sob story about no longer playing football, how school and grades really didn't matter, and that I had no future plans at the moment. At every juncture in the presentation Ms. Butler interrupted me to make sure she thoroughly interpreted the words that were coming from my mouth. At the end of my presentation she said, "William, you are presenting again the next class period and I don't want to hear a symphony of sorry again." The next class period I was the first to present. She called my name and asked, "William, are you ready to play the violin?" "The violin?" I replied. "Yes, speak a melody that will bring harmony to your life." When I approached the front of the class, I could feel the eyes from my peers staring at me. No one was ordered to give a second presentation except me. I can recall starting my presentation with the phrase, "I feel sorry for myself because . . ." Before I could get the "myself" out, Ms. Butler said, "William, you can sit down. You are presenting again the next class period." My attitude was very nonchalant. I really didn't care. I was thinking that I'd get up there and still begin the presentation the same way.

The next class period, I entered in a suit. This was a complete reversal of my previous attire. I normally wore blue jeans, white t-shirt, and Reebok classic tennis shoes to class. I know Ms. Butler and the class believed that I wore the suit to impress them; however, I didn't. The truth was that I didn't have any clean clothes to wear. I would have just worn the suit slacks but the ensemble looked better with the coat. I even splashed on a little cologne. The quirk of fate was that the response I received from them motivated me to give an enlightening presentation about how my past was not a predictor of my future and I was taking a new approach to education. I focused my discussion on school and grades. I made a declaration that I would come to class on time, sit close to Ms. Butler in our assigned circle seating, pay attention, and not write rap songs all class period. Oh my God, Ms. Butler held me to every word.

She was teaching me an invaluable lesson. This was a tough lesson for a 19-year-old to comprehend. American publisher, Malcolm Forbes, once stated, "Too many people overvalue what they are not and undervalued what they are." Ms. Butler could have let me feel sorry for myself. Yet, she didn't. She challenged me to become a better student. I took two classes with her that semester. I received A's in each class. The only A I had received prior to that was in basketball my first semester at NSU. To Ms. Butler, I thank you: my life is now the perfect melody.

How to (Favorably) Impress Your Professor

When universities first started, there were no grades and no diplomas. You went to Plato's Academy or Aristotle's Lyceum because you wanted to learn. When you had learned all you wanted, you left. Unfortunately, things are no longer so pure. University students, generally speaking, want a degree, and preferably a degree with honors, not one where you just scrape by with mediocre grades. So, presumably, you the student want to impress your professor favorably. After all, he or she will be grading you in the course, and with professors as with future employers, impressions do count. There is some degree of subjectivity in all assessments, and if you have impressed your professor as a lazy, apathetic, complaining, slacking, or hostile student, this will likely affect the professor's evaluation of your work. So here are some basic and, I hope, helpful tips in how to make a good impression on your professor.

1. Communicate
If you have a serious problem that is going to affect your performance in the course, speak frankly with the professor about the problem. If a work or family situation is making you miss class, be chronically late, or not get assignments in on time, explain the situation to the professor, and he or she will almost always be willing to make a reasonable accommodation. Professors know that people have to live life as well as attend their classes, and that all sorts of emergencies come up—as well as tyrannical bosses, illness, deaths in the family, divorces, drug and alcohol problems, etc. Communicate the problem honestly with your professor (very personal details do not need to be divulged, of course). Tell your professor about problems as early

in the term as possible. If you perform poorly in a course and approach the professor at the end of the semester with what sounds like a weak excuse, you will not receive much sympathy.

2. Attend Class

The most consistent advice you will receive from a professor is to attend class. Attend class at all cost. Even if your professor does not officially require class attendance, numerous unexcused absences look bad. Skipping class suggests that you just don't care or that you clearly think you have better things to do with your time. Most professors care deeply about what they are teaching and have put a considerable amount of effort into learning difficult subjects and slowly and painfully learning how to communicate that knowledge to students. When you don't bother to show up for class, your professor reads this as indifference towards his or her expertise and effort. I once had a student come up to me after class to tell me that he would not be there for the next three weeks and then proceeded to ask me if I was going to be covering anything important. Hint: If you have spent five to ten years of your life in graduate school learning something, you are probably going to think it is important. In the 1978 comedic movie, *Animal House,* actor Donald Sutherland plays a literature professor who responds to student's apathy with the cry "Hey, this is my job!" Teaching you is part of your professor's job, and he or she probably feels that it is a pretty important job.

3. Ask Questions

Again, your professor probably thinks that what he or she is teaching is important and interesting. People always respond favorably to people who show an interest in what interests them. A professor is complimented and gratified by an expression of interest on the part of a student. Not every kind of question will favorably impress your professor; however substantive questions related to the lecture will do the job. Some kinds of questions will backfire and create a really bad impression. I don't mean "stupid" questions, but questions that honestly express a failure to understand some parts of the lecture or resonates that a student is not paying attention. The majority of professors appreciate it when students who do not understand ask for clarification. There is no shame whatsoever in asking for further clarification; it is shameful to settle for ignorance.

4. Use Good In-class Manners

A class is not your social hour. Don't spend it whispering and giggling with your neighbor. Such childish behavior should have been left behind in the fourth grade, and any self-respecting professor will deeply resent it when it occurs in his or her class. Pay attention, or at least act like you are paying attention. Don't go to sleep in class. Don't eat meals in class. Having a snack or drink is OK with most professors, but it is not appreciated, to say the least, to try to lecture to a student who is stuffing his or her face. More importantly, be courteous and do not participate in social media usage. For instance, do not check Facebook, Instagram, Twitter, Snapchat, and Youtube. Whatever you do, please do not hold a text message discussion while the professor is lecturing to the class.

Professor Keith M. Parsons
University of Houston—Clear Lake

University of New Orleans (UNO)

I later returned to Louisiana and attended the University of New Orleans (UNO). Ms. Butler had planted in me a confidence I had never had before. She encouraged me to expand my mind and never go back to where it was and become more by working to develop myself. She urged me to follow the A.B.C's of life: be A.ssertive, be B.old, and be C.onfident. I took that attitude with me when I enrolled at UNO. In the first semester, I took four courses and finished with a 2.5 G.P.A. A couple of semesters had passed doing B- and C+ work. I was determined to improve as a student but didn't put forth 100% effort. In order to become a better student, I needed to attend class regularly and overcome my poor study habits. It was time to adopt new studying methods. The demands of the courses became more rigorous. I employed the following strategies:

1. *Developed a study schedule.* It was necessary to identify the time of day that I was most alert and blocked at least two hours to study.

    What is your study schedule?

    _____

    _____

2. *Chose a study environment.* Initially my study environment was the apartment. It later became the library and coffee shop.

    Where is your study environment?

    _____

    _____

3. *Organized study groups.* After the first exam, I would recruit the students with the highest scores to participate in a study group.

   Do you participate in study groups? Are they effective or ineffective?

   _____

   _____

4. *Have a strategy to avoid wasting time.* Before I studied, I mapped out a strategy to designate the amount of time spent on each subject.

   Do you have a strategy to avoid wasting time? What is your routine?

   _____

   _____

5. *Have a pen, highlighter, and stack of note cards.* These items were essential to effective studying. I used the pen to take notes on what I reading. This aided in reading actively. Next, to reinforce the information, I used a highlighter. This helped to recall main headings and important concepts. Last, I made note cards for definitions and chapter questions. Each of these methods helped to retain information.

   Is there a pen, highlighter and stack of note cards in your book bag?

   _____

   _____

The major turning point of my academic success came after having a long conversation with one of my best friends, William Bolling. We were both in similar situations having attended multiple schools and now ready to graduate. Will said to me during the conversation, "Man, it's time for me to graduate and move along to the next phase of my life." I agreed and asked what was his plan. "First, I need to get my butt in the library and study consistently," he responded. I concurred. Will then suggested that we go to the library Monday through Thursday to study for at least two hours. I replied, "Monday through Thursday? Two hours?!," to make sure I heard him correctly. I agreed to the plan, not confident that we could keep it up. I wasn't sure that

I had the discipline to follow through with such a commitment but I was determined.

In the beginning, it was easy to go to the library Monday through Thursday out of necessity. I had seven courses and needed to buckle down to pass them and raise my G.P.A. After the first round of exams I wanted to ease up and not go. I had to be mindful of the inner voice within that said to continue and be disciplined. Will and I set goals to study, make good grades, and graduate. In fact, it was me that told him, "We can't slack off and stop going to the library." Even on days when we didn't have homework or completed assignments early, we still stayed for the entire two hours either reading or studying ahead. We both were more determined than ever to become model students. At the end of that semester I had a 2.845 G.P.A. The discipline Will and I exuded in that semester set the groundwork for my commitment to graduate in a timely manner.

My next step was to visit the academic advisor and get an exact total of the number of credit hours left to graduate. The only problem was I had changed majors multiple times while in college. At NSU, I never declared a major. During my time there I took random classes that I heard were easy in hopes of raising my G.P.A. and staying eligible to play football. At OCC, I was a sociology major and took courses pertaining to that subject matter. At UNO, my major changed several times from sociology to psychology to finally general studies. When I met with the advisor in the psychology department and informed him of my self-imposed graduation date, he suggested that if I wanted to graduate in that time frame to seek a degree in general studies. This sounded perfect to me. At the onset I thought taking courses in the general studies curriculum would be easier than courses in other disciplines. I was wrong. Therefore, I had to maintain the same level of discipline formulated from the study pact I made with Will.

When I met with the academic advisor in the general studies program, Dr. Gifford, we devised an academic plan that would allow me to graduate ASAP. He told me that I had a total of 40 credit hours left, 13 three credit hour classes, and one lab. Finally, I could see the light at the end of the tunnel. In the meeting, he asked me, "What are you going to do after you graduate?" My answer was, "I don't know." What I realized that day was I didn't have a plan, a strategy, or a sense of purpose. I thought that graduating would be like reaching the mountaintop but it was only a step on the ladder of success. Before I left the office, Dr. Gifford left me with a saying from French author and journalist, Albert Camus, "Life is the sum of all of your choices."

After the meeting with Dr. Gifford, I was set to enroll for the summer semester. That summer I took three courses and finished with a 2.910 G.P.A. I took seven courses in the fall (3.105 G.P.A.) and four in the spring (3.184 G.P.A.) to complete my degree in general studies. I finished undergraduate with a cumulative G.P.A. of 2.934.

During this whirlwind academic year, I took the graduate record examination (GRE) for graduate school admission and scored over an 1100, which was a respectable score. I applied to a number of criminology and criminal justice programs. My goal was to have options. I knew I was graduating with a general studies degree and subpar G.P.A. My family and friends were proud of me after I graduated but I was not proud of myself. I realized that I was not living my dream. I was not living my dream because I didn't have one and was afraid to fathom one. Applying to graduate school was premeditated by doubts and fears that had become my worst enemy. The summer after I graduated, I received an acceptance letter in the mail from Florida State University, which was one of the top criminology and criminal justice programs in the country. Off to Tallahassee, Florida, I went, ready to "attack this [challenge] with an enthusiasm unknown to mankind!"

Racial Discrimination at Florida State University (FSU)

American author Josh Jamison once wrote, "There comes a time when you have to choose between turning the page and closing the book." This quote defined my overall experience at FSU. I entered the criminology and criminal justice graduate program confident and eager to learn and left discouraged and feeling incompetent to achieve academic success at a high level. The first semester at FSU started out well but ended on a sour note after I received a failing grade, B–, in a course I carried an A in the entire semester. I challenged the grade and it was overturned citing some discrepancies in the grading procedures. The following semester I had also received subpar grades in courses I believed I should have made an A in. Despite the grading issues, I overcame them and graduated with my Masters degree in one academic year.

From the beginning of my stint at FSU, I heard former and current African-American graduate students talk about the covert racial discrimination from some of the professors. Quickly, I realized which professors they were referring to. However, because they taught required courses I could not avoid them. There were only four African-American graduate students in the entire program including myself. Only one at the time had completed course work and taken comprehensive exams. She failed both sections the first time and one section the next. In spite of everything that was happening around me, I still believed I could prevail over any adversity I experienced.

In my first semester in the Ph.D. program I took all required courses. This was important because coupled with the courses I took during the Masters phase; I was eligible to take my comprehensive exams in my second semester of the Ph.D. phase. I had only been at FSU for a year and half and was already preparing to take the Ph.D. comprehensive exams. It seemed like yesterday, I was in Dr. Gifford's office and he asked me, "What are you going to do after you graduate?" And I replied, "I don't know." Now, I was about to take the Ph.D. comprehensive exams.

The Ph.D. comprehensive exams were organized in two parts: (1) criminological theory and criminal justice and (2) research methods and statistics. They were two separate eight-hour exams. The first time I took the exams, I passed the research methods and statistics part and failed the criminological theory and criminal justice part. How could this be? When I asked my advising professor to review the results, she told me that I had failed the criminological theory and criminal justice portion by a small margin. To add, two members on the committee, tenured white males, indicated that I had memorized the material and were not sure I was able to adequately conceptualize criminological theory. These two professors had failed me on every section of the exam when other professors either gave me a high or low pass. When I voiced my concerns to my advising professor, she recommended I take the exam again to display my knowledge on criminological theory. She was very supportive and encouraging.

Disappointed from failing that portion of the exam, I wanted to meet with my advising professor again and voice a couple of major concerns. She was Canadian, openly gay, untenured, and didn't quite grasp the visceral racism that existed in the South.

Although she certainly understood and experienced discrimination, it was difficult for her to fully know the practicality of covert and systematic racism. To make matters worse, the two white, tenured, male professors that failed me on the comprehensive exams were not fond of her lifestyle. And here I was a 24-year-old black male, dressed in hip-hop attire every day, and slightly over-confident, taking his Ph.D. comprehensive exams.

Concern number one, I believed I was being penalized for speaking out in class against some of the blasphemous comments these two particular professors would make. And the other concern was that the comprehensive exams were supposed to be anonymous; however, they weren't. She gave me a spirited talk, assured me that she would do everything she could to support me, and I proceeded to prepare for the next round of comprehensive exams scheduled in five months. I again failed the criminological theory and criminal justice portion of the exam. This time I failed by a larger margin.

Besides my advising professor, there was very limited support from other faculty and administrators. I developed a rapport with the Dean, however, he made sure to be a mediator rather than taking sides. He had fielded complaints about these two professors in the past, but refused to intervene. There was only one black professor in the department but he did not have tenure thus too afraid to even offer advice. Ironically, he graduated from the same program, experienced much of the same covert racial discrimination, sought outside counsel to address the issue of racial discrimination in the program, FSU did a direct hire of him for an assistant professor position, but he still refused to take a stand regarding the issue.

During this period, I was teaching one course at FSU and another at Florida A&M University (FAMU). I mentioned the situation to my class at FAMU couched in a lecture on institutional racism. Ten years later, while teaching at Wichita State University, I received the following email from one of my former FAMU students:

> Hello Dr. Hoston,
>
> *I met you a few years ago when you were a doctoral student at the School of Criminology and Criminal Justice [at Florida State University]. I was a student, at the time, in one of the courses you taught at FAMU. At the time, you and I talked about your experiences at Florida State, trying to navigate your way through the racial pitfalls of being a black student in the School of Criminology and Criminal Justice.*
>
> *I now find myself where you were then—I've finished my course work. A few weeks ago I took comp. exams and my major professor, a black professor named [John Doe], informed me last week that I failed both parts of the exam. He was on the [criminological] theory committee, but not allowed to vote or comment when my exam came before review! He said that if he were allowed to vote he would've passed me. This is disturbing because the exams are supposed to be graded anonymously and I was placed at a disadvantage without a major professor to argue on my behalf. In addition, the reasoning provided to me for my failure was that my answers on both exams were not "in-depth" enough to show that I really understood the material. The answers were correct, mind you, but not in-depth enough. And this vague reasoning does not satisfy me.*
>
> *I am sending a certified request for a copy of the original comments on my exams. But, in doing so, I thought about you and your similar experiences. My experiences in the department have suffered as a result of isolation and a lack of mentorship. I have many stories to tell about things I've experienced. But I wanted to write you to get advice on how I should proceed from this point as well as insight into what led you to leave Florida State.*

Reflecting on this student's email, I feel as though I let them down. After I failed the criminological theory and criminal justice portion of the Ph.D. comprehensive exam twice, I left FSU and took a corporate job at MCI WorldCom in Cary, North Carolina. As I said earlier, I left discouraged and feeling incompetent to achieve academic success at a doctoral level. Who was I to earn a Ph.D.? Just a few years ago, I had no plan, no strategy, and no sense of purpose. Now, I had Bachelors and Masters degrees. Was this the ceiling of my academic achievements? Had I already reached my full academic potential? These were certainly greater academic achievements than any of my family and friends. Maybe I should have turned the page and fought rather than close the book at FSU.

Finish What You Start!

Prolific motivational speaker Les Brown states, "People don't fail because they aim too high and miss, but because they aim too low and hit!" When college students lower their academic expectations it can be damaging to their psyche. There is nothing great about making a bunch of "C's, D's, and F's. To me that means, "C.ouldn't D.ecide F.uture, and thus low expectations evolve coupled with negative self-talk. Too many times college students victimize themselves with negative self-talk. In freshman year, students may not be determined enough or understand the work ethic needed to achieve good grades. When they make average grades, they develop negative self-talk that leads to "comforting attitudes" as described in Chapter 1. Other excuses I hear students make are, "I was not really interested in that course." Or, "The teacher is boring." Each time I will counter with, "You can learn useful information in every class. And, despite how boring you perceived the teacher to be, you can always learn from them." After they look at me like I'm crazy, smile, and say, "You're right, Dr. Hoston," we proceed to develop strategies for them to improve their grades. Before they leave my office, I give them a piece of paper that reads, "Excuses are tools of the incompetent, that build bridges to nowhere and monuments of nothingness. Those that use them seldom amount to anything."

At times, negative self-talk can translate into negative energy. The result is that this can lead some students to want to drop out of college. For example, Chris was a former student I taught at Wichita State University that wanted to quit school. He was a sixth year senior. All his friends had graduated and found a job. Every time I saw him and asked how he was doing, he would reply, "I'm making it. Just trying to graduate. I've been here forever." I'd offer encouraging words and tell him, "Keep working hard. Degrees don't have dates on them, just your conferring school, degree program, and name." He'd always thanked me for the kind words and promise to continue to work hard to complete his degree.

One day Chris entered my office and said he was considering dropping out of school. I had never seen him that discouraged. Again, I began to give him encouraging words. In the midst of our conversation he asked, "Dr. Hoston, why do you have so much confidence in me?" I answered back by saying, "Everyone needs someone to believe in them. Somewhere from freshman year to now, you lost the passion to excel academically and graduate. You have to gain that back. Success is a journey defined by your level of determination."

How do college students learn to eliminate negative self-talk after "failing moments"? How do they maintain a high level of self-confidence to continue in school? How do they stay inspired to not H.ave A.nger T.oward E.veryone R.eaching S.uccess (H.A.T.E.R.S.)? What Chris did was continue the journey to graduate from college. He did, however, drop out that semester but returned with a renewed focus. Dropping out of school was his failing moment. He realized it was difficult to receive the job he desired without a college education. Next, he began to take ownership of the poor decision-making that led him to make bad grades that was the root of lowering his self-confidence. Last, he stopped comparing himself to his friends that had already graduated. He stopped being content with living his fears and began living his dreams. Chris finished with a degree in sociology and went on to graduate school. Today, he is a senior vice president at the Boys and Girls Clubs of America.

What is Your G.reatest P.ersonal A.chievement (G.P.A.)?

After working for a mere eight months in corporate America at MCI WorldCom, I returned to the University of New Orleans (UNO) to finish my Ph.D. The seed of achieving a Ph.D. had been planted, and I refused not to have this goal sprout from a lack of determination. UNO didn't have a Ph.D. program in criminology and criminal justice. It was a choice between the urban studies or political science programs, and I chose the latter. I had never taken a political science course in my life. The summer before classes started, I read several books to gain a background on the subject. When people would ask why did you switch from criminal justice to political science? And my answer was always, "To make myself more marketable."

Simultaneously, while beginning the Ph.D. program, I also began teaching at Xavier University of Louisiana (XULA) as an adjunct professor. Known for its history of educating black students in the sciences and placing them in medical school, XULA was an inspirational place for me to be teaching. I confided in my colleague who is now my mentor, Dr. Ronald Dorris, professor of English and African-American history and culture, about the trials and tribulations of FSU. His advice was straightforward, "William, you have to finish that Ph.D." He noticed my passion, love for teaching, and willingness to mentor college students. But, he kept saying, "William, you have to finish that Ph.D." What he really was saying was, get your membership card to continue to do something you love to do.

I started off slow in the Ph.D. program at UNO. Making all B's the first few semesters. A ton of reading on some subjects I was unfamiliar with and depressed sitting in courses I had taken before like research methods and statistics. The past experience from FSU was haunting me. Soon I began to question myself. The ability to achieve academic success was lying dormant in me and needed to be activated. I had to rebuild my confidence and listen to the inner voice that said, "Quitting is not an option." In time I overcame the depression and began to improve academically in the program.

I was near completion of my coursework and comprehensive exams were quickly looming. I approached the exams with the same fervent nature as I did at FSU. This time the outcome was different. I passed each section with high honors. Finally, I saw the finish line to completing the Ph.D. My major professor and I had settled on a dissertation topic and a projected completion date was in sight. Everything seemed to be going as planned until Hurricane Katrina ravaged the city of New Orleans.

Hurricane Katrina was another major setback in my pursuit of obtaining a Ph.D. I set out to evacuate from New Orleans and travel to Atlanta, Georgia, until the hurricane passed. But, when the storm was over it had flooded 80% of the city of New Orleans and much of the university was damaged. UNO temporarily shut down and uncertainty began to seep in. During this period, I traveled from New Orleans to Atlanta, to Dallas, to Houston, to Baton Rouge, and back to Houston, all in an attempt to check on displaced family and friends and then make certain that the school would reopen to resume completion of the Ph.D. Eventually, I settled in Houston, Texas. That stay only lasted six months.

From Houston, I took a visiting assistant professorship position at Wichita State University in Wichita, Kansas. This was a tremendous social adjustment for me. After the first semester, I was ready to leave. Although I enjoyed teaching at WSU, I missed my family and friends. Plus, hanging over my head was the need to finish the Ph.D. and put that chapter of my life behind me.

The flooding of Hurricane Katrina also damaged my major professor's home. He was now residing in Atlanta, Georgia, and we were working on the dissertation by email and fax. Teaching courses and long hours of working on the dissertation took an emotional toll. Through this difficult time, I remembered what my mentor, Dr. Dorris, would repeatedly say, "William, you have to finish that Ph.D." This period in time taught me how to take control of my own destiny. I worked day and night, night and day. From time to time, my days ran together. That was how determined I was to finish the dissertation. In the words of the great Civil Rights leader Rev. Dr. Martin Luther King, Jr., "The ultimate measure of a man is not where he stands in moments of comfort and convenience, but where he stands at times of challenge and controversy." Despite the sum of my academic setbacks I remained optimistic. Determination gave me the resolve to keep going. Hall of Fame baseball great Tommy Lasorda often said, "The difference between the impossible and possible lies in a person's determination."

On graduation night, it all came together. When the announcer called my name, "William Terrell Hoston," my major professor placed the Ph.D. hood on me, and I heard my family and friends cheer for me, it was all worth it. The day itself was surreal. After the graduation, I handed my Godmother the degree and cried in her arms. I had come a long way from having a 1.929 G.P.A. after my first semester in college. To date, receiving the Ph.D. has been my G.reatest P.ersonal A.chievement.

NAME _____   DATE _____

Questions for Personal Growth

1. What are your short-term educational goals? Write them down and achieve them.

2. How determined are you to achieve academic greatness? Will you work day and night, night and day?

3. What are your long-term educational goals? Write them down and achieve them.

CHAPTER FOUR

The Road Less Traveled Can Lead to Success

"The Window of Opportunity."

I have been staring through this window all my life / Gazing beyond the pane / Leaning against the seal / Looking for tranquility

From time to time / I place my head out of the window / To clear my mind / Hoping it blows a wind of courage

Sometimes the wind blows in an unfamiliar direction / But in that direction / I choose to go down a path of the unknown / Praying it will take me to a place I've never been before / For a newer and richer experience

Hoston (1998); *written after a professor at Florida State University told me I wasn't Ph.D. material.*

Courage

AMERICAN ESSAYIST AND POET RALPH WALDO EMERSON WROTE, "Do not go where the path may lead, go instead where there is no path and leave a trail." This quote is dear to me because every since I began teaching, I have strived to leave a trail of encouragement in the lives of every college student I've had the opportunity to teach. Students come from all walks of life. The common thread among all students is that they need someone to believe in them. Newton, a student I had the pleasure of teaching twice at UHCL, was one I greatly attempted to leave a trail of encouragement in his life.

Newton took two courses with me, legislative process and LSAT prep. In each course, he excelled academically. In legislative process, he came to class on time, completed assignments, wrote a fabulous research paper, and performed well on all exams. He was only mediocre during class discussions. Newton seemed nervous and unable to gather his thoughts at times. One day, I told him to speak up and be confident in his responses during class discussions. After class, he apologized for not being able to fully explain his position on the topic. I gave him some encouragement from social activist, Maggie Kuhn, that said, "Speak your mind, even if your voice shakes."

Two semesters later, Newton enrolled in my LSAT prep course. The first week, the class took a full practice LSAT exam. The second week, we learned about the law school application process, financial aid options, and began to formulate outlines for students' personal statements. I require each student to stand in front of the class and read what they have written thus far. This exercise is used as a method of bonding for students to establish relationships. I want each student to hear what circumstances have driven the other to want to attend law school and be encouraged by the others' life journey. When it was Newton's turn, he read the following to the class:

> I was born in Ocotlan, Mexico, in 1989 to a Mexican-American father and a Mexican national mother. For the first two years of my life, my parents observed me as a healthy infant. However, I was not healthy. Doctors in Mexico couldn't diagnose what was wrong with me. My parents then decided to move to the United States so that I could have a better quality of life. In the United States, I was diagnosed with Bannayan-Riley-Ruvalcaba syndrome (BRRS). While this is a serious condition, it does not interfere with my ability to live a healthy life. I do however need to receive regular physicals.
>
> A major question I've always had was why was I born with this syndrome? This question is not a spiritual one, but a literal one. I have asked this question to many genetics doctors. Most have said it was due to some unpredictable force, while others gave the possibility of an outside source mutating my parent's genes. For the longest time, to be honest, my syndrome did hang over my head. It is not easy as a child to know that at any time a malignant tumor could be growing inside of you. What hurt more was not that I might die, but that I really wasn't given a chance to live in the eyes of many doctors. I have learned to embrace BRRS and use it as a tool of motivation in my academic career.

After Newton finished reading his personal statement, all the students in the class applauded for his transparency. Many were amazed by his courage to remain positive in spite of this obstacle in Newton's life. He did not allow his health issues to hinder his academic progress. He is much like Eric, who I described in Chapter 1. They both exemplify courage. Newton and Eric have faced adversity in their pursuit of academic excellence but have not allowed their physical condition to defer their dream.

Five Tips to Prepare College Students for Academic Success

On many occasions college students enter my office and ask how they can prepare themselves for academic success. Most of time they are freshmen who are intimidated by the transition from high school to college. Other times, they are sophomores and juniors that still have not figured out how to handle the academic rigors of college. By the time they come to my office their confidence is deflated and courage gone. I stress to them the importance of being proactive in their approach to academic achievement. It is imperative for students to take action despite their fear of failure. Fear will open doors of insecurity that are difficult to close. Courage will be the only thing that closes those doors.

In many cases, professors will give students tidbits for academic success such as: (1) make sure to attend class, (2) study a lot, (3) join student groups, and (4) be confident in your academic skills. For most students, this is very good advice. As well, there is additional advice that can be disseminated to students to prepare them for academic success. In the following text, I present five tips. Students who employ these practices should experience a higher level of academic success.

1. Have a Positive Attitude about Learning

Students should have a positive attitude about learning. A student's attitude toward learning often dictates how well he or she will perform in class and how much information will be retained. Students should approach each class, even those not in their major, with a positive attitude. A serious misconception of many students is that some courses are not essential to their learning process. In all courses, it is key for students to: (1) be an active listener, (2) take good notes, (3) participate in class discussion, and (4) meet with the professor during office hours if clarification of lecture notes is needed. Students must exude a positive attitude at all times.

2. Don't Be Late, Sit in the Front of the Class, and Pay Attention

Don't be late to class. Sit in the front of the class and pay attention to class lecture. In class, the first impression is the most important impression. Students are encouraged to be on time for class and recognize the significance of punctuality, presence, and attentiveness. They should approach class like a business meeting, where promptness, attention to detail, and retention of information is central to success. As the old adage goes, "On time is late and being late will get you fired." Also, a professor will notice the student that sits in the front. Students that sit in the back may not be in the best sightline of the instructor; being in the immediate sightline of the instructor acts as a cue that the student is paying attention and interested in the subject matter.

3. Participate in Class Discussions

Students should make sure they participate in class discussions. It is imperative that students listen to peer interaction and partake in the class discussion. One way to move in this direction is to routinely ask the professor questions for clarification. Do not be a nuisance. But, rather, ask questions of substance and add critical thought that is valuable to the discussion. This will lead to an exchange with the professor and exhibit your interest in the subject matter. Professors want students to be engaged in the lecture and this is a significant way to demonstrate that.

4. Don't Be Afraid to Visit the Professor's Office

Don't be afraid to visit the professor's office. Professors enjoy talking to students who take an interest in their courses. Make sure to visit: (1) early in the semester and (2) during office hours or set an appointment. This will often lead to the professor knowing the student's name, that the student is excited to learn about the subject matter, and identifying that the student is committed to making a good grade in the course. Students should be self-initiating in the learning process. Professors will view this as a sign that students value their education.

5. Be Sure to Obtain a Good Academic Advisor

Students must obtain a good academic advisor. A good advisor will: (1) make sure students have chosen the appropriate major, (2) ensure that students are taking the necessary courses to graduate, (3) provide career assessment and future planning, and (4) give mentorship and support. Choosing a good academic advisor is essential to achieving academic success. Because academic advising is an ongoing process from freshman to senior year, students need to align themselves with advisors who understand their educational goals.

TABLE 1

Do's and Don'ts Checklist to Achieve Academic Success

Do's	Don'ts
Maintain a positive attitude.	Begin a negative attitude.
Begin each day with a promise to become a better student.	Look for excuses not to excel in the classroom.
Be determined to work hard.	Give a subpar effort in your courses.
Know why you are in college.	Sabotage your college experience.
Take 12–15 credit hours each semester.	Drop below full-time status unless absolutely necessary.
Set clear academic goals.	Continue to take courses without a blueprint for academic success.
Go to class on time, sit in the front and pay attention to class lecture.	Arrive at class late, sit in the back and fall asleep.
Participate in class discussion.	Be afraid to participate.
Visit the professor's office early in the semester.	Be reluctant to visit professor's office.
Make sure to obtain a good academic advisor.	Wait to get academic advising or continuously change advisors.
Study hard to achieve good grades.	Settle for average grades.

Why Plagiarism Makes Me So Angry

Students don't do many things to make me angry. I didn't even get mad the time the guy came up to me after class and asked "Hey, I'm going to be out of town the next three weeks. Are you going to be talking about anything important?" I don't get mad when students will disappear for two months and then show up with a flimsy excuse. I didn't even get mad the time the student was scheduled all semester to make a class presentation on a given day and then skipped out because his grandma visited. I do, however, get mad when students plagiarize. Very mad! A student one time whined that he did not think he deserved to fail my course for plagiarizing on just one paper. I responded that I did not think he deserved the punishment either but that failing him was the worst thing the university would let me do to him. If I had my way, plagiarists would be tarred and feathered and ridden off the campus. Just joking. Here's why plagiarism makes me so angry:

1. Plagiarism Insults My Intelligence
There is a scene in *The Godfather* where Al Pacino, playing the part of Michael Corleone, confronts a turncoat. He says, "Don't tell me that you are innocent. That insults my intelligence and makes me very angry." That is precisely my reaction when I catch someone plagiarizing.

I generally do not impress people as a stupid person. I have two earned Ph.D.'s, have published several scholarly books, and used to be a member of Mensa, the "high I.Q. society." Yet, plagiarists clearly think that I am a dimwit. They believe that I cannot tell the difference between their writing and the writing of an expert. When they copy an expert's writing and present it as their own, they clearly think that I am too dumb to notice. Ahhh, but I do. There is a world of difference between the writing of the plagiarist and someone who knows something. The difference is like night and day to anyone who has been teaching at the college level for thirty years as I have. Or maybe the plagiarist thinks that I am too stupid to track down the sources they copied. But if you can find them, I can find them. And I will.

2. Plagiarism Shows Contempt for Other Students
Most students work hard for their grades. They burn the midnight oil, balancing jobs, kids, spouses, and the thousand-and-one other demands on everybody's time. They come to class and participate, even though after a full day they would love to take a nap. Most students act responsibly. When they make a good grade, they have truly earned it.

The plagiarist doesn't work hard nor sacrifice. He or she lets someone else do the hard work and they just copy it and get the reward. If they get by with their plagiarism, they get the good grades just the same as those who deserve them. Piece of cake! Hey, theft has many advantages over honest work! It has so many advantages that cheating might just become a habit. If you can rationalize cheating on your grades, you won't have too much trouble convincing yourself to cheat your employer, your kids, or your spouse. You might just cheat your way into unemployment, a divorce, or jail someday!

3. Plagiarism is Theft

When you take someone else's academic work and present it as your own, you are stealing from that person. And it is a particularly odious kind of stealing. Believe it or not, academic work is hard. You have to spend long years learning abstruse things and master the even harder task of learning how to express your knowledge and insights effectively. Every published work is like the tiny tip of an iceberg, with a vast bulk of reading, thinking, and painstaking composition below the surface. When, after years of preparation, delayed gratification, and intense, focused work, you do produce some publications, what is your reward? Money? Hah! Your reward is the honor of others—scholars and students—who read your work and credit you for teaching them something and making their intellectual lives richer.

The plagiarist who steals your work for his or her own unearned benefit steals something of much deeper significance than one who steals merely your wide-screen TV or jewelry. That student steals your dedication, your sacrifice, your creativity, your intelligence, your passion, your love and inspiration—not to mention your sweat and tears. The student does it because he or she is too lazy or apathetic to do the work for themselves.

4. Finally, and Worse of All, Those Who Plagiarize Betray an Utterly Twisted and Debased Concept of the Whole Academic Process

The pursuit of knowledge is a noble thing. It is one of the few unalloyed goods that humans pursue. Each university and college, for all of their faults, has professors who possess a pure dedication to the discovery and transmission of knowledge. Learning is part of the basic purpose of human life; it is one of the reasons we exist. It is good for its own sake, whether it produces any material gain or not. The pursuit of knowledge is a holy and beautiful ideal.

The plagiarist spits in the eye of that ideal and drags it through the mud. For the plagiarist, academic requirements are just a hurdle to get past, a hoop to jump through, or an impediment in the way. Being required to think and write for yourself is absolutely essential for the pursuit of knowledge. For the plagiarist, though, it is just an inconvenience. Learning is just an obstacle, so you do what you have to do to get around that obstacle. If a paper is standing in the way of your enjoyment, you just copy it. If a test is standing in your way of passing the class, you just look over at the other student's paper. Hey, it's all B.S. anyway, the plagiarist thinks, so why spend any time on it? If cheating will get you the grade you need, and the time for the important stuff like drinking beer and hanging out with friends, why do the work?

Your professors have dedicated their lives to a noble ideal. When you treat it with utter contempt and disrespect the academic values that we have lived for, are you surprised at our anger?

Professor Keith M. Parsons
University of Houston—Clear Lake

LGBTQ Students Tips for Success

Transitioning to college for LGBTQ students can be a really intimidating process. In many respects, it may be the first time you're away from home and now are completely on your own; living, functioning, and identifying outside of your normal circle as either a Lesbian, Gay, Bisexual, Transgender, or Queen student. The majority of colleges are great at creating a welcoming environment for all students, and have developed a greater understanding of LGBTQ issues and concerns on campus. Here are three tips for success for LGBTQ students:

1. Check Out the College's Non-Discrimination Statement
This should be listed in the college's brochure or on their website. Make sure that it mentions explicit verbiage related to not discriminating on the basis of sex or sexual orientation. It is imperative that the college strives to maintain a safe and inclusive campus environment for LGBTQ students.

2. Find LGBTQ Resource Centers
It is important to explore what LGBTQ resources exist on campus. Do they have an LGBTQ Student Services Office? Do they have an LGBTQ Student Services Coordinator? Does the college offer Safe Zone Training programs for faculty and staff? Is there a Gay-Straight Alliance on campus? Does the college have an LGBTQ studies program? All of these questions speak to fostering an accepting environment for LGBTQ students and whether or not the college will be a good fit for you.

3. Talk to Other LGBTQ students
When you are seeking a college to attend, at the campus orientation ask about LGBTQ resources and what offices house LGBTQ services for students. Observe if there is a place where students can meet, discuss, and voice their LGBTQ issues and concerns. Ask can you talk to, or can they introduce you to, other LGBTQ students before making a decision to attend their college. If you are already a student on campus, find the LGBTQ networks from the tips above. Connect with other LGBTQ students in the quest to build positive, supportive relationships.

Shaun R. Simon, LGBTQ Ally

The Cuban Four

As mentioned earlier, I first began teaching at the collegiate level at 23 years of age at Florida State University (FSU). The opportunity to begin teaching at such a young age allowed me to develop my craft and formulate effective teaching strategies. I quickly realized that the goal of all educators should be threefold: (1) they should want to inspire students to become critical thinkers, (2) to become lifelong learners, and (3) in the end become better people. The ultimate gratification for an educator is making a difference in students' lives.

I first started teaching as an assistant in a criminology course while working on my Masters degree. In the class, the main professor taught a student body of around 400 students and three teaching assistants facilitated small workgroups to reinforce information learned in the larger forum. After receiving my Masters degree at FSU, I was assigned to a course as the sole instructor. That course was entitled "social problems of youth." Initially, I was extremely nervous about the idea of teaching the course. On the other hand, I was confident in my ability to prepare an intellectually stimulating course that students would enjoy. I approached the course with a fanatical work ethic and brought an enthusiastic attitude into the classroom. I was blessed to have a group of students that were hard working and resilient in their quest to achieve academic success. The enrollment of the course was approximately 25 students. Almost two decades later I have kept in contact with about 12 of them until this very day. Of the 12, none stand out like the "Cuban Four." They are Joey, Ralph, J.C., and Dave. These four Cuban young men went to FSU as ordinary students and left as extraordinary men on the path to career success.

Their journey together began early in Miami, Florida. They were childhood friends from Cuban decent. After graduating from high school, Joey, Ralph, and J.C. attended Miami Dade Community College (MDC). Dave was the oldest. He first attended Florida International University (FIU) and almost failed out after his freshman year. He later joined the rest of them at MDC. Close to their graduation, Ralph encouraged Joey to attend FSU. Then, J.C. and Dave followed suit. Off they went to FSU ready to face a brave new world.

They were all different, but each complemented the other. Joey was the level headed one. He was the typical college student, worked hard but not hard enough at times. Ralph was the smartest, but certainly did not apply himself. I reprimanded him the most. J.C. worked the hardest and made the best grades. He was quiet but fierce. Dave was nonchalant about school. He was content with a C. His philosophy was C's equal degrees. I scolded him from time to time as well.

In the social problems of youth course, I encouraged each student to take the Kaplan practice GRE or LSAT exam for extra credit. Although most students took advantage of this option merely to improve their final grade, the underlying goal was to motivate each student to seek an advanced degree beyond their undergraduate studies. Joey, Ralph, J.C., and Dave took the practice LSAT exam. None of them did particularly well on the exam. Nonetheless, I encouraged them to consider law school as an option in their academic endeavors. The seed was planted. Afterward, all I had to do was water their intellectual roots. They grew to giant heights.

These days, Joey is a managing partner at a prestigious law firm in Orlando, Florida. After graduating from FSU, he attended Stetson University College of Law. Ralph is an attorney at a known law firm in Miami. After graduating from FSU, he contemplated many options before deciding to attend St. Thomas University School of Law. J.C. is an associate attorney at a prominent law firm in Miami. After graduating from FSU cum laude, he attended St. Thomas University School of Law. He went on to become a student leader where he was elected president of the Student Bar Association. Dave is a vice president at a major insurance company. After graduating from FSU, he went to St. Thomas University School of Law for one semester, but reconsidered and chose a different career path.

The main reason that they achieved academic and career success was because each used the other as a source of motivation. The positive alignment of their friendship was paramount in achieving success. Each possessed the same level of ambition or higher. None of them deviated from the ultimate goal. I cautioned them to keep their circle of friends close knit. I emphatically told them to only hang with others that thought like them, dreamed like them, and wanted to succeed like them. Their friendship was driven by a core respect for each other. Over the years, I have grown the closest to Joey; however, I keep the rest very near to my heart. I always tell current students about the "Cuban Four" and how their bond helped propel them to success. When I think of them I get overwhelmed with joy and happiness.

Letter from Joel "Joey" Piedra

Dear Will,

    I hope this letter finds you doing well. I am writing you after great thought of the impact you had on my life. I recently had an opportunity to reflect on my life and ponder how far I have come. I can honestly say that you are a major reason for my success. I can recall my first semester at Florida State University. I walked into your class, social problems of youth, on the third floor of the Bellamy Building with my three good friends, Ralph, J.C. and Dave. The irony of that day is, I never thought that my future mentor and good friend would be the professor teaching the class. That semester you gave me the courage to take a practice LSAT for law school. Afterwards, I told you my horrible score. I still relive the conversation as if it were yesterday. You said to me, "Joey, you still need to take the LSAT and apply to schools. You will make it. I believe in you." That day changed my life. I was a student with very little focus and ambition. At that point in my life, I was just trying to find myself.

    The next semester, I took your victimology course. I enrolled in this course because I not only enjoyed your social problems of youth class but I found comfort and motivation in your teaching style. After that semester, we continued to communicate and became friends. We have been friends for nearly fifteen years now. You have attended all the important events in my life. You were at my undergraduate ceremony, law school graduation and my wedding.

    I am now the managing attorney at my law firm. I have been a practicing attorney for 8 years. You gave me the courage to pursue a goal I never believed I was smart enough to achieve. Throughout the years, you have instilled in me the courage, work ethic, leadership and motivation I needed to succeed. The entire time you were still a mentor and good friend. For that, I thank you.

In closing, the words I write you today cannot completely describe how you have changed my life. Thank you my dear friend. Keep up the great work. I one day hope to have the special ability as you do to change students' lives. Like I always tell you, God brought you into this world to motivate and change lives.

My Greatest Student

Dear Joey,

You are by far my greatest student. It's not because you were my smartest student. It's not even because you worked the hardest in my classes. It's because after I encouraged you to achieve your dream, you continuously encouraged me to achieve my own. As you know, I left Florida State University after I failed my Ph.D. comprehensive exams. I was discouraged and felt incompetent. It was you that told me to be strong and go finish the Ph.D. somewhere else. While many people were telling me the same thing, you also made me realize it was important to finish the Ph.D. by explaining to me how I had affected your life and that I needed to continue to do the same for other students.

Throughout the years, when I would get discouraged and wanted to quit teaching and change my profession, it was you that would ironically call out of the blue and begin telling me how much my presence meant in your life. When I would tell you of my plans, you'd always say that if I stopped teaching I'd be doing a disservice to future students that needed professors like me. At times I have struggled with the notion, "just because you are good at something does that mean that you are meant to do it?" And the answer is, "Yes!"

You helped to give my life a sense of purpose. Your belief in me made me realize that I couldn't just speak the message of courage, I had to be courageous and finish my Ph.D. I needed to overcome my failing moment at Florida State University and push forward. In the words of former British Prime Minister, Winston Churchill, "Courage is going from failure to failure without losing enthusiasm." You kept me enthusiastic about wanting to help to impact other students' lives, as you said I did your own.

Student Testimonies of Courage

American author Mary Anne Radmacher once wrote, "Courage doesn't always roar. Sometimes courage is the quiet voice at the end of the day saying, 'I will try again tomorrow.'" The following courageous testimonies are from former students during their educational journey. Please read them to find courage and inspiration in their life's journey.

The Law of An Abundant Life

Growing up in a large family has undoubtedly shaped my character. Though I was the second born of six children, I was the first female. My father was extremely old fashioned and felt it necessary for me to oversee the caretaking of the younger children as well as preparing dinner and keeping the house tidy. I also managed to hold down a full time job, participate in numerous extracurricular activities, while maintaining exceptional grades in school. I was very close to my younger siblings and had a bond with them that most of our mutual friends envied. Upon graduating from high school, I enrolled in college and was very excited to begin the next chapter in my life. That excitement ceased when I became involved with an abusive boyfriend and lost focus in my schoolwork. After three semesters in college, I decided I needed a new beginning and moved on from that relationship as well as from school. I told myself that I would return to college when I restored order in my life.

A couple of years later, my younger brother became extremely depressed and chose to take his own life. I cannot begin to explain the devastation it caused to my family, especially my mother. Trying to understand suicide is like being stuck inside of a maze with no escape. I felt confused, lost and began to question the meaning of life. I did not understand how I could move on without my brother by my side. With the help of my family, friends and numerous books, I was able to look at my situation in a different light. I saw my experience as an opportunity to live to my fullest potential. I felt a sense of urgency to accomplish my goals. A month after his death I enrolled back in college. I was determined to finally obtain my degree. For the next couple of years I worked two jobs, attended classes and maintained a decent G.P.A.

The rest of my family seemed to deal with the death of my brother in a similar manner. The other siblings became more involved in their own academic and career goals. My father, however, was unable to find a method of coping with the loss of his son and fell into a deep depression. He became addicted to alcohol and pain medication as a means of dealing with his sorrow. Shortly after, my father took his own life as a result of my brother's suicide. This was the most defining moment in my life. I was extremely saddened to see my father pass away in the manner that he did. I realized that while I could not control the fatal choices of both my brother and father, I would have full control of the way I responded to these situations. I vowed to continue with my academic goals and make my mother proud.

To uphold the promise made to my mother, I completed my undergraduate studies and began law school. Midway through the first year, I knew I had made the correct choice. I also knew that my brother and father were smiling down keeping me encouraged, motivated, and steadfast in my academic journey. I have overcome many obstacles in my life. An important quote I recall when faced with new obstacles is by Frank A. Clark that states, "If you can find a path with no obstacles, it probably doesn't lead anywhere."

Angelina Wike
Attorney

The Young Girl With the Beautiful Smile

Hello fellow students, my name is Jennifer Alexandria Bannister-Yarde. I was born on August 25, 1987, in Galveston, Texas. Six months after my birth, I was diagnosed with Neuroblastoma in my left kidney and had to receive an emergency bone marrow transplant. Neuroblastoma is a very rare form of cancer that develops from immature nerve cells. It usually is found in children age 5 or younger. The news that I had cancer devastated my mother. The doctor provided her with two options: Put me on prescription medication to reduce the pain or allow me to go through chemotherapy treatment. My mother chose treatment.

After my first round of chemotherapy treatment, the doctors realized I had lost my hearing. In addition to the loss of my hearing, other underlining health issues surfaced such as memory loss, speech impediment, and having a low immune system, making it hard to fight off illnesses. These medical setbacks had a big impact on my social development. In particular, it took me longer than most children to learn how to read because I could not hear.

My mother eventually put me in speech therapy sessions when I turned two-years-old. Instead of sending me to preschool and kindergarten right away, I continued with speech therapy sessions. These sessions ended when I was six years old. My mother believed I was ready to begin school. In the classroom, I understood the materials being taught by the teachers. The only problem I had was that I couldn't read clearly. I did not truly begin reading clearly until age seven.

My speech therapist, Mr. Barefield, played an instrumental role in my social development. He was my speech therapist from age two to 18. Mr. Barefield pushed me to my limits. This was done because he observed that I had the ability to improve my speech and it not be a hindrance to my life, academic, or career success. He reinforced what my mother had always told me, that I was normal like other children.

My mother, Angela Burnett, is my rock. She has always told me I was child of God. All my life, she spoke positive words that thrust my will to overcome early medical setbacks. She came to the United States in the 1980s from England to pursue her Bachelors of Science in Nursing at the University of Texas Medical Branch (UTMB) in Galveston Texas graduating top of her class. The age of seven is symbolic in our lives because that was the age I began speaking and the time she graduated from nursing school. She set the foundation for my life. First, she put me in speech therapy sessions. Second, she refused to heed advice to put me in special education. In the summer, instead of playing outside everyday like other children, I went to summer school. On the weekends, I would be inside practicing how to read and write. Most importantly, she filled me with positive words because she believed in my ability to overcome my speech impediment.

My mother demanded that my brother and I do something with our lives. She wanted us both to be leaders and not followers. Her tough lessons have stayed with me. As a result, I worked hard to become a good student. The journey was not without trials. In college I took countless remedial courses and it took five years to complete my Associates degree. Despite early difficulties, after the Associates degree I finished my undergraduate degree in two years. It took a total of seven years, but I finished. I recently graduated from the University of Houston—Clear Lake in criminology and now attend graduate school in sociology. My goal is to work with at-risk youth and be a positive, motivating force in their lives.

From the day I was born, my mother has been grooming me to be strong, resilient, and to understand that one day my personal story could be used to influence the lives of others. Besides my mother, I dedicate this journey to two important people. First, my late brother Jonathan Campbell Bannister-Yarde, who died in a tragic car accident, I miss him dearly. Last but not least, my amazing son, William Addison Moore, who is my world. When he was born, it made my life important and gave it a renewed purpose. I thank God for all of the positive people in my life; past, present, and future.

I am grateful for the trials and tribulations that I have endured. Each experience has molded me as a person. I have grown so much over the years. Today, I can look at myself in the mirror and smile with great confidence. The reflection of a beautiful smile.

Jennifer Alexandria Bannister-Yarde
Educator

From Janitor to Future Ph.D.

My journey is unique to say the least. I went from being a janitor to now a Ph.D. student. My upbringing began in a poverty stricken city in the south, Pine Bluff, Arkansas. While small in population, per capita, Pine Bluff has been mentioned as one of the most dangerous cities to reside in the United States. It has drawn comparison to other southern cities with a high rate of crime such as Memphis and New Orleans. For most black males, that typically spells a life marred by structural and cultural factors that limit opportunities. In other words, it is very easy to become a statistic.

If one is able to avoid the street life, there is the dichotomy of obtaining an education to achieve success or fall in line with an oppressive thinking that the only other options of success within the city are tied to becoming a professional athlete, rapper, or dope boy. Luckily, in the end, I chose education.

Growing up, I navigated through the dysfunctional maze of being black, fatherless, born into poverty, and at times feeling like there was no hope for my future. At certain intervals, I had to deal with times of homelessness. With God's grace and mercy, I came out of the maze not in prison or dead to eventually land in college.

I was a freshman in college when I came to the point of enlightenment that I wanted to be better than my past circumstances. I was determined to become a successful black man. With this frame of mind, I knew I had to head down a path of the unknown. I was determined but afraid of this newfound passion to become successful. I desperately needed a way to pay for my academic studies. I applied for countless jobs to no avail. I finally took a full-time position as a janitor at a local junior high school. As a result, I was a full-time student by day and full-time janitor by night. My time working as a janitor was not easy, in fact it was quite a difficult and humbling experience. While I did not want to work as a janitor, I had to in order to achieve my goal of graduating from college. As Dr. Hoston stated in Chapter 1, I humbled myself to the situation and/or experience to achieve the goal. I eventually went on to earn my Bachelors degree in mass communication at the University of Arkansas at Pine Bluff. Following a stint working in broadcast production, I then earned my Masters degree in journalism and public relations from Arkansas State University.

Even though the road to achieving academic success has been difficult and humbling, the payoff in the end will be worth it. Currently, I am a doctoral student at West Virginia University. From reading my story, I challenge undergraduates to never give up. As you move forward in your academic journey, I'd like to share the following tips:

1. You Don't Have to Follow the Traditional Path—For many people, following the traditional path in life is not necessarily the path to travel on your journey to success. When working as a janitor, many of my friends would always ask, "Why are you working as a janitor? You are never going to become successful working a crappy job like that!" Little did they know, that without the job I probably would have never graduated from college. It provided added fuel to my desire to become successful.

2. Approach Life With Fearlessness—In my eighth grade science class, I learned that fire is its hottest when it has a blue hue. From that day forward, I knew that I wanted to approach life with the intensity of that blue flame. When I was a janitor, I became determined to be the best janitor at the school. I stripped, buffed, bleached, and waxed floors so well that I won the coveted janitor of the year award! Yes, this may be a minimal award to some, but it was what I became in pursuit of achieving this accomplishment. I learned that no matter the job, if you approach it with a fearless sense of professionalism, a thorough work ethic, and a commitment to do the best job possible, it will render positive results. That applies whether you are a janitor or president of the United States.

Hopefully, my journey "From Janitor to Future Ph.D." has inspired you in some way. Yes, the road less traveled is not easy, but it is not impossible! Pursue your greatness one step at a time and never give up!

Shaun M. Anderson
Professor

Child of Destiny

When students walk into my office, there is a picture of Wendy L. Couser. The picture is there because of two reasons: (1) she has the most amazing story of faith, hope, and determination of any of my students in the last two decades, and (2) she inspires me. I love her dearly.

Hi, my name is Wendy. My story is one of faith, hope, and determination; my faith in God, hope in humanity, and the determination to overcome all obstacles that may cross my path. Coupled with a deep conviction to honor God, each of these has kept me going when I believed life had given up on me. I am sharing my story in hopes that whoever reads it will gain the faith, hope, and determination to overcome the trials that may enter their lives.

At the age of ten, I was kidnapped and raped. The effects of this tragic incident forever changed me. I became emotionally unstable, mentally homeless, and sought refuge in the most obscure of places, people, and things. When a child is sexually assaulted, they need understanding and support. I received neither. I felt as if I wasn't wanted or loved anymore. No one understood my internal sadness. During this period, the only person in the whole world I wanted to love me, my father, despised me. The sadness made me not want to live anymore.

Prior to this tragic incident, I was a happy child. I was born in 1961 to a young couple in a small town in the mountains of Pennsylvania. My father was in the Army and my mother had yet to graduate from high school. They married before I was born to give me my father's last name. I was loved very much by my family and adored by my grandparents. My Grandmother was grounded in the Christian faith, her faith and belief in God passed on at a young age has carried me through the most trying times in my life. I needed God to look over me because from age 10–19, I was raped multiple times, physically and verbally abused by my father, shown limited love and affection by my mother, lived in several juvenile detention centers, graduated from high school at 16-years-old, sexually abused by one of my boyfriends, had gotten married and divorced, spent a short time as a prostitute, and conceived a child. Then later, I went to prison for drug distribution.

The first time I was raped resembled any other day. However, on the way home from school a man approached and told me that my father had asked him to come get me to attend a party in his honor. I went with the strange man, but once we arrived at the destination there was no party. The man took me to an apartment somewhere in a small town close, but not far from the Army base we lived on in Germany. The details of this space and time of my life are foggy, but I do know I was held for a great length of time and was raped by multiple men. I assume the men eventually grew tired of holding me. They returned me close to my home and dropped me off in a remote area. The effects of the rape propelled me to attempt suicide several times. I was a shell of my ten-year-old self. I wasn't the same little girl I was before I was taken.

Because of what happened to me, my father received military orders to return to the United States. He became very angry because he wanted to remain in Germany. This led to him drinking even more. While I had seen his temper and aggressive nature in the past, it became worse over time. When he drank, he was an angry drunk who became very violent. That violence was directed toward my mother and me. These episodes eventually pushed me to befriend people who would allow me to spend the night at their house to avoid being around my father when he was drunk. Befriending random people correlated at times to making bad life decisions. I met some good and bad people along my journey to find salvation.

My parents grew weary of trying to cope with my erratic behavior. Never acknowledging that they were partly to blame for the dysfunctional nature of my life. I eventually landed in a youth detention center. There I did my school work and made all As. The teachers were amazed at my academic abilities. Within a year I had completed all the course work to satisfy the requirements to graduate with a high school diploma. At the age of 16, I graduated with my high school diploma from this youth detention center. This was a proud moment because at that time I was the youngest girl to have ever accomplished this academic feat at the center. On graduation day, I was very excited. After the ceremony, I expected to return home and planned to talk to my parents further about attending college. The teachers at the center expressed that I had the academic potential to graduate from college. I communicated this to my parents in our phone conversations. The teachers made going to college seem like a real goal.

My mother attended the graduation with my younger brothers and sister. I didn't get the opportunity to talk to my mother and siblings before the graduation. That was okay because I knew I was going home afterwards. I had already packed my belongings and was ready to go. When it was time for me to walk down the aisle, all I could do was smile and grin in pure excitement and joy. Going home afterwards was all I could think of as I walked past my family in the audience to receive my diploma. My father did not attend, however, I had come to grips with the fact that he didn't love me anymore. Finally, when graduation was over, I got up and went over to my family. I hugged everyone and told my mother I was going to take all of my belongings to the car. She let me leave, but while I was taking my things down to the car, the administrator and counselor came to inform me I was not going home because my father did not want me to return. I remember thinking how could a father do this to his child who had worked so hard to not only graduate, but to seriously think about going to college. On one of the happiest days in my life, I was resuming my stay at the center, re-entering the admittance process feeling like a misfit. I had not done anything wrong, why were they locking me up on the happiest day of my life? How could they do this to me?

From that point on, there were a myriad of trials and tribulations in my life. Mostly trials, as I sought refuge in men that sexually, physically, and verbally abused me. However, one day as I was walking down the street, a young woman pulled up and asked if I wanted a ride. I took the ride that would forever change my life. During that time, I was down and out. A boyfriend had raped me again; I had married and divorced, spent a short time as a prostitute, and conceived a child. The young woman's name was Melissa; and she took me on a trip to find a higher power. We became friends. I confided in her. She invited me to church, and I said yes. I thought that if I were ever going to find any stability in my life, it would come from God.

Even in the midst of seeking the approval of God, I relapsed to my old ways. In need of money, I agreed to sell marijuana for a big time drug dealer in the area.

Friends had told me it was not a good idea. Being stubborn and determined to make money, I did it anyway. Every Wednesday I went to church with Melissa and sold drugs all the other time. One day, the door to the home where I was staying burst open and the police came in full force with guns drawn. While the police were cuffing me, all I could do was say "thank you God." The police were in shock and wanted to know why I was thanking God. I told them that now my journey with God was to begin. I was liberated. I ended up taking a plea bargain instead of going to trial and was sentenced to a 3 to 10 year sentence in the Kansas State Prison. That didn't bother me; I just wanted to begin the next phase of my life's journey.

After my release from prison, it still took some time for my life to get on track. I had several more children out of wedlock until I finally decided to pour all my love into my children and attend community college. After attending community college for a short while, I met a man, Darryl, who would become my life partner. Like me, Darryl had spent some time in prison and had just gotten out when I had met him. In the beginning, Darryl was supportive of my academic endeavor, but would later make comments as to me dropping out of school, or he would say that I was too old to go to college, or better yet college was going to be a waste of time because I desired to major in criminal justice and my degree would never land me a job because of my criminal background.

I completed several years at the community college before I transferred to Wichita State University (WSU) in Wichita, Kansas. In the spring of 2009, I graduated with a degree in criminal justice. Graduation was great. I was so proud of myself when I walked across the stage. I was excited to go into the real world and put my degree to work. However, life after graduation was stagnant. I could not find a job. I applied but to no avail. I was even angrier that Darryl was proving to be right. I was not going to find work in my field because I had a criminal record.

Dr. Hoston, one of my mentors, had left WSU. In our correspondence, he advised me to pursue my Masters degree. I was accepted into the Masters program in criminal justice at WSU. I graduated in a two-year period. This time after graduation I was confident that I was going to get a job in the criminal justice field. I took the appropriate steps to make sure I could obtain employment. First, I applied for clemency with the Governor of Kansas. I prepared all of the necessary paperwork. I had to drop off the packets of materials to the Kansas Department of Corrections parole review board (the board that oversees all clemency applications). Then I had to go to Junction City, Kansas where my crimes were committed to drop off other documents. For almost a year, I waited to be granted clemency. I applied for a job working as a Juvenile Intake Officer through Harvey County Community Corrections. In the past, I had applied for other jobs there but was never hired. I went on the interview and it went well. After a week, I called the supervisor. When she answered there was excitement on the other end of the line. The supervisor informed me I had received the job and could start immediately. I was screaming in my head, "Yes!"

Reflecting on my life, God has allowed for me to go through a lot of really tough experiences, so I could learn from them and use them to reach others. Today, I understand that being raped multiple times as a youth led me to become a prostitute. I now understand why I have multiple children by different men. I now understand why I was always in search of someone to love me and always ended up being alone. It took years of therapy to become confident in myself and to know that I can do anything I set my mind to do. Every day I am blessed to be around people who can learn from my story. All the trials in my life were not in vain. They have molded me and now allow me to sculpt the lives of others.

Wendy L. Couser
Survivor

NAME _____ DATE _____

Questions for Personal Growth

1. What is your testimony? Write it down. Use it as a source of motivation.

2. Do you have the courage to overcome the perils of life? Will you take action despite a fear of failure?

3. Theologian and author Eric Butterworth said, "Don't go through life, grow through life." Are you *going* through life or *growing* through life?

CHAPTER FIVE
Being Content Opens the Door for Failure

"The End Result."
(Abbreviated Version)

I have a sign on my back that reads, "Save me!" / Not from white racism or black prejudice/ But from unadulterated insanity

You have to be crazy to get out on the front line of life / And fight to educate this generation/ So call me crazy!

When I walked across the stage / I freed a million slaves / That's the impact / I want to have on this generation / When you walk with Christ / You can step out on faith

I know that failure is opportunity in disguise / That's why I wear a mask to scare off these haters / Our deepest fear / Is that we are powerful beyond measure

If you don't work day and night to achieve success / Then your thinking is off the wall / Beat it!

I was birthed to educate minds / Nothing in this world / Is more dangerous than sincere ignorance

Hoston (2011); *written to inspire college students.*

Perseverance

POLITICAL ACTIVIST BERNADETTE DEVLIN IS NOTED FOR SAYING, "Yesterday I dared to struggle. Today I dare to win." Throughout life I have attempted to persevere through the hard times and stay motivated. Even those that motivate others still need motivation at times. What has kept me motivated has been a desire to find specific tangible things that I could focus on when my will to continue had diminished. There have been times during my journey where life has challenged me to focus on the goal at hand. F.O.C.U.S. means Follow

My Late Grandmother

My late grandmother, Mildred Hoston, was a former educator and dedicated woman of Christ. She told me more positive things than anyone in my life. My grandmother was always upbeat and reassuring. Her favorite saying to me was, "Boy, when you grow up you gonna be somebody." She encouraged me to read the Bible and find inspirational materials that feed my soul. One of her favorite inspirational readings was "Our Deepest Fears" by author, Marianne Williamson. Her favorite excerpt from the passage was the following:

> *You are a child of God.*
> *Your playing small does not serve the world.*
> *There is nothing enlightened about shrinking*
> *so that other people won't feel insecure around you.*
> *We are all meant to shine, as children do.*[1]

On November 4, 1997, my grandmother passed away at Phoebe Putney Memorial Hospital in Albany, Georgia. She died in my first semester of graduate school at Florida State University. It is difficult to put into words the impact that her death had on my life. My greatest support

---

[1] Williamson, Marianne, *A Return To Love: Reflections on the Principles of A Course in Miracles*, (Harper Collins, 1992, pgs. 190–191).

O.ne C.ourse U.ntil S.uccessful. To overcome these challenges, I have maintained a cerebral train of thought on one particular person, one specific thought, one exact goal in life or my overall life's contribution.

I have found three specific tangible things to focus on to keep me motivated: (1) My late grandmother, Mildred Hoston, (2) My internal belief that I can achieve anything I put my mind to, and (3) My conviction that I was placed on this earth to help others.

system was now gone. She died of Alzheimer's disease, the illness that leads individuals to lose their memory and bodily functions, eventually causing death. Albany, Georgia, is only a two-hour drive from Tallahassee, Florida. On my off days from attending class and teaching, I would go and visit her in the hospital. Oddly enough, although Alzheimer's disease led her to forget most of her family and friends, she still remembered me. One of my many nicknames is Sweet Boy because of my love for candy as a child. When I'd walk into her hospital room and say, "Hey grandma," she'd ask, "Is that you, Sweet Boy?" "Yes ma'am," I'd reply. During our conversations, she would often have a lapse in memory. Yet, I was grateful that she still remembered me. While visiting, at times she would say, "You need to finish your degree. And make sure to leave those fast girls alone." I would answer back, "Grandma, I already have one degree, I'm working on the Masters degree now." Her response was, "Baby, get all the degrees you can. Don't stop until you have the highest one."

At my grandmother's funeral I compared her to former slave and American abolitionist, Harriet Tubman. Over an eight-year span, Harriet made 19 trips to north Philadelphia from the Deep South leading over 300 slaves to freedom. My grandmother was much like Harriet Tubman. She adopted my father, had several foster children, worked with the mentally disabled and handicapped to ensure that they had basic necessities and their bills were paid, and performed her weekly church duties. The passing of my grandmother was not only a loss for me, but also a loss to many people that relied on her services, support, and love. I miss her dearly.

My Influence

Before they closed the casket / I made a promise to my Grandmother / That I would take my mind out of the gutter and place my head in the books / So I wouldn't be another young black male statistic

I became engaged to education / And we eloped on a philosophical journey / Since that day / I haven't cheated on her one time / With a basketball, a football, a baseball, an 8-ball or a microphone / Check 1-2, 1-2

The last time I broke the rack / The cue ball flew off the table / That is how bad I want to scratch my place in his-story

When they placed the Ph.D. hood on me / My hood began to believe in me / I blew a wind of courage to diminish the flames burning from the cross in my front lawn / I then realized that my life would be O.KKK / I placed my Bible on the ground / And I stood on top of the word / To God be the glory!

Source: William Hoston

I Can Achieve Anything

In the movie, "The Pursuit of Happyness," Will Smith's character Christopher Gardner tells his son, "You got a dream. You gotta protect it. People can't do something themselves, they wanna tell you, you can't do it. If you want something, go get it. Period." This quote embodies the idea that parents need to instill in their children the belief that they can achieve anything. My grandmothers, mother, and Godmother were influential in this process. They fed me with words of affirmation and helped to build self-confidence. These women kept me motivated. They knew that if I stayed highly motivated, I would be more likely to achieve academic and career success. Like Ms. Butler I talked about in Chapter 3, they held me accountable. Collectively, they provided encouragement and guidance, while allowing me to be my own individual. They preached humility, but also told me to be great, be amazing and be awesome.

On the last day of class each semester, I give students a speech telling them that they can be anything they put their minds to. My message to them is to be great, not mediocre. I ask them, "Are you committed to greatness or mediocrity?" At the end of the speech, I tell them the story of, "The Pillow." The pillow knows all of your dreams, goals and aspirations. It also knows your deepest thoughts, fears, reservations, and doubts. The pillow knows if you're confident, courageous, gutsy, and willing to persevere through the tough times. It has felt your tears of frustration and disappointment. More importantly, it knows if you have any fight left inside of you to continue the journey toward academic and career success. The pillow knows the truth. I close by telling them, "Realize your dreams and accomplish your goals. Don't leave your life on the pillow."

A former student at UHCL wrote me the following email:

> Dr. Hoston,
>
> My father has a nickname for me, that although I loathe, it's pretty accurate. He has named me, "The First Lady of Quit." He calls me that because growing up, instead of sticking things out; I have easily acquiesced to the fear of failure. I don't truly know nor can explain "how" or "why" I exult this feeling of inadequacy at times, but this has been apart of my personality.
>
> When I graduated with my Bachelors degree, I was blessed to have a 3.7 G.P.A. that gave me options for pursuing a graduate education. I was ecstatic to graduate with such a high G.P.A. because it showed me that I wasn't this weak, fragile individual that quit at every juncture, but rather, was a determined student eager to prove that I could make A's. With a little push from my professors, I was able to raise my self-esteem and succeed in the classroom. Sometimes, I hate the way that I am because I allow myself to become inert and give in to my fears and trepidations. Well, this is the case now. I am currently in a graduate program, but my true passion is to become an attorney. However, I am afraid of taking the LSAT exam. If I receive a low score that will be a determining factor in deciding my career path. I want to take the next available LSAT, but once again, I feel that cold, gripping fear that always consumes me when important decisions need to be made in my life.
>
> Before I started this email, my initial question to you was, how do I break out of this pattern and move forward? However, while writing I began to reflect on the many motivational stories you told us in class. I then thought

back to the story you told the class on the last day. It was the story of, "The Pillow." I must admit, my pillow has felt a lot of tears. Trying to figure out life, as a college student, can be difficult and overwhelming at times. Nonetheless, I have persevered and leaned on my family and friends for support. The all-knowing pillow has been my soundboard. As you always said in class, "Work hard and don't make any excuses." I still have that piece of paper you handed us on the first day of class that read, "Excuses are tools of the incompetent, that build bridges to nowhere and monuments of nothingness. Those that use them seldom amount to anything."

I told my father to rename me, "The First Lady of Hard work." My goal is to not allow my fears to overcome my will to succeed. Instead of crying in the pillow, I will begin to pray in the pillow and ask God for strength to conquer my fear of failure.

Placed On Earth to Help Others

Ever since I was a child, I have always been reared to help others. This stems from my grandmothers, mother, and Godmother. Each of them were "givers." At all cost they would attempt to help those that were less fortunate or those that simply were going through difficult times. They instilled in me the value of helping people. In many of my motivational lectures, I conclude by stating, "I am the son of Mildred, Bertha Mae, Thelma, and Janet, they birthed me to help change the world."

In the words of Indian philosopher and leader Mahatma Gandhi, "Be the change you want to see in the world." In my opinion, in order to become an agent of change, there are two specific courses of action an individual must take. First, you have to become the message. In order to deliver the message of change, an individual must become the message. People will respect an individual for attempting to live their life by the principles they preach. Although many of us fall short at times, it is important to strive toward adhering to that goal. Second, you have to identify a purpose larger than your own individual desires. It is important to understand that helping others ultimately contributes to your own self-gratification and provides an abundance of joy.

For example, after I began teaching, I cried at every graduation I attended. Initially, I would try to conceal the tears. After several graduations

I allowed the tears to flow. I have come to recognize that I cry at every graduation because I love to see people achieve their goals. People are born to achieve. It is a great feeling to witness a student approach the graduation stage, hear their name called aloud, listen to their family and friends cheering from the audience, receive their diploma, and see the exuberance on their face. That is a captivating moment that brings tears to my eyes. These moments are especially gratifying when that individual was a former student. To see their growth from freshman to senior year, observe them be courageous during failing moments, persevere to achieve academic success, and watch them prepare for the real world is an amazing feeling. French poet Guillaume Apollinaire encapsulates this moment perfectly, "Come to the edge, he said. They said: We are afraid. Come to the edge, he said. They came. He pushed them and they flew."

A great American philosopher George Bernard Shaw wrote the following passage in a letter prefacing his book, *Man and Superman: a Comedy and Philosophy*. The passage characterizes my experience as a college professor. It is the ideology I ascribe to when it comes to helping college students achieve their goals.

> *I am of the opinion that my life belongs to the whole community and as long as I live, it is my privilege to do for it what I can. I want to be thoroughly used up when I die, for the harder I work, the more I live.*[2]

Graduation Check List

1. Apply for Graduation ☐
2. Finish all Final Exams ☐
3. Make Sure You Do Not Have Any Financial Holds ☐
4. Purchase Commencement Notifications ☐
5. Inform Family and Friends ☐
6. Order Your Cap and Gown ☐
7. Attend Commencement ☐

---

[2] Shaw, George Bernard, *Man and Superman: a Comedy and Philosophy*, (Penguin, 1989, pg. viii).

Post-Graduation Check List

1. Have an Updated Resume and Cover Letter ☐
2. Identify Three Professors Prior to Graduating to Write Future Letters of Recommendation ☐
3. Apply for Jobs in Your Career Field ☐
4. Obtain Copy of Official Transcripts ☐

Five Tips to Achieve Career Success after Graduation

Every May and December before graduation, I get a rush of students that come to my office looking for career advice. Most of the time, I wish they had come earlier to ask for advice because these soon-to-be graduates are often in a frenzy about the thought of facing the "real world." For those that have planned poorly, when June and January roll around the emotional high they were on during graduation has come crashing down. In spite of their poor planning, I encourage them to stay motivated to either seek an advanced degree or find a comfortable fit in the job market. The major transition from college to the "real world" can cause stress and anxiety for some students. It is important for students to persevere through this phase and work toward achieving their postgraduate goals. Below are five tips for graduating students to practice to achieve career success.

1. Be In the Moment

Graduating seniors should be in the moment. Plan your work and work your plan. Decide what your goals will be after graduation. Don't wait until your senior year of college. Set goals that will enhance your quality of life. Give serious consideration to the goals that will be most beneficial to assist in your long-term endeavors. Create a list and map out the specific steps to accomplish the goals. Go to a career counselor, advisor, or professor and talk about career plans. If you are pursuing an advanced degree, take the required standardized exam, maintain a high G.P.A., apply before the deadline, and ask for letters of recommendation from professors and employers. If you are interested in obtaining a job after graduation, make sure to have a well-crafted cover letter and resume.

> *"If you don't live in the moment, you'll watch your life pass 'goodbye'."*
> ~William T. Hoston

2. Make Good Decisions

Students need to make good decisions by eliminating poor thinking and decision-making. Not making a decision is making a decision. Make decisions and follow through with them. More importantly, do not be afraid to detour from the decision if it does not most benefit you. However, make sure you have exerted 100% effort on the decision made. If change is necessary, be flexible. There is nothing wrong with beginning anew or starting over. Change to improve your current circumstance is absolutely good. Be prepared for the unexpected. If you are open to change sometimes more opportunities may emerge.

> *"Always remember that the future comes one day at a time."*
> ~Dean Acheson

3. Build Strong Networking Relationships

Develop healthy relationships with individuals by networking, either with those in the community, internship, or your current place of employment. This is a great way to build contacts, disseminate information, and possibly meet leads for jobs. Meeting new people is easier for some than others. However, be confident it will be worth your time and energy. Possibilities are endless when you come in contact with individuals that can help you reach your goals. People are always willing to help bright and ambitious students. Network, network, network!

> *"Success isn't a result of spontaneous combustion. You must set yourself on fire."*
> ~Arnold H. Glasow

4. Be Accountable for Your Actions

Please be accountable for your actions, faults, and successes. It is important to own up to your mistakes. Will you make mistakes? Yes. But, you can learn from them. Individuals will gain more respect for you. It is also vital to claim your accomplishments. Be humble and identify those that have helped you accomplish your goals. To achieve the goal of being accountable for your actions, students should do the following: (1) Be an active listener. This will help to avoid mistakes. Do not be a know-it-all. (2) Listen more than you talk. Those that know the ropes will provide tidbits and tricks of the trade to help you become successful.

> "When the dream is big enough, the odds don't matter."
> ~Dexter Yeager

5. Continue to Believe in Yourself

Have a deeply rooted disposition that you can achieve anything. Learn to say repeatedly to yourself, "I can and I will." I believe it is important to live in a state of mind of "when" not "how" or "if." Telling yourself "when" suggests that you can and will. On the other hand, telling yourself "if" or "how" cast doubts and reservations. For example, "when" I get accepted into graduate school or "when" I get this job, sounds confident. In contrast, "if" I get accepted into graduate school or "how" will I be competitive in the job market, seems to cast doubts about your ability. Don't put a limit on the possibilities of what you can do or achieve. Be confident in your abilities. We live in a global, competitive environment, which means you've got to stand out from the crowd to get ahead.

> "In order to succeed, we must first believe that we can."
> ~Michael Korda

What Do You Want to Be When You Grow Up?

Most students can recall how older adults, particularly our family members, would ask the common question, "What do you want to be when you grow up?" As with most young children, the standard answers, at that time, are teacher, doctor, lawyer, firefighter, or police officer. Today, you might get some of the same common answers, but with an added fairy tale ending thrown in the mix. When I was asked this question at a young age, I would respond with embarrassment the phrase "maybe a doctor." I had no idea at that time what I wanted to be. The pressure was too great to make a life decision at six-years-old about what I would become by age 25. As you can imagine, my dad, an Army Sergeant Major, and my mom, a banker, were extremely proud to hear my future ambitions at six-years-old. Thus, at an early age this career goal became a heavy "torch" that I had to carry throughout my entire educational journey. My parents would tell family and friends that I was going to be the first doctor in the family. The pressure became enormous and the fear of failure and letting them down was even greater. During my senior year of high school, I participated in a work-study program at the local top-notched medical school. I then was accepted into one of the state's top universities as a Pre-Med, scientific nutrition major. The groundwork was being laid for me to go to medical school. However, I had no more desire to become a medical doctor as a freshman in college than as I did at six-years-old.

Throughout this part of my educational journey, there was this churning in the pit of my stomach, my heart was empty, and my vision was unclear because I knew becoming a medical doctor was not what I really wanted to do with my life. I did know that I loved the college environment and what it had to offer, especially the many different people I had the opportunity to meet and befriend. As I continued on with the degree plan and this path of my college journey, I went through all of the motions that go along with being admitted into medical school. I first took the Medical College Admission Test (MCAT), applied to a few schools, and kept up the outward appearance that it would all work out. As you might guess, I did not do so well on the MCAT, but I can say I was proud to be among those who attempted the examination.

In the fall semester that I was scheduled to graduate with my Bachelors of Science degree, I finally mustered enough courage to tell both my parents and *myself* the truth—*had no desire whatsoever to become a medical doctor.* A few weeks before graduation, I sat them both down and explained that I was not going to medical school, and I never wanted to become a medical doctor. My dad calmly asked what I wanted to do with my life. Before I could form the words to verbally express my thoughts, he completed the sentence. He said, "You want to be a teacher, don't you?" I replied, "Yes, sir!" It was at that moment that the churning in the pit of my stomach stopped, my heart was filled with a new ambition, and my vision to obtain career success became clearer. I exhaled and then cried tears of joy. They both respected my decision to head toward a different career path. Throughout my life, all I had ever wanted to do was to make my parents proud. While I love them to death, it was emotionally unhealthy for me to continue on a journey that had been partly orchestrated by others who thought they had my best interest in mind.

After I graduated, it was my dad who came across an advertisement about an Alternative Teacher Certification Program at the very university that I had just received my degree. I applied to the program and was accepted. I began that spring semester and got my first teaching assignment the following fall, in a city about an hour and half drive from my parent's home. My first year as a teacher was difficult. I had only one education course under my belt. However, teaching was my passion. I knew it was my gift. Once I started it became clear that it was what I was suppose to do with my life. I was nominated for the First Year Teacher Award at that school; unfortunately, I was not eligible to receive the award if I had won because I was not yet certified.

One night a week, I travelled to the university to take a course to complete my goal of becoming a certified teacher. I did this for two years in addition to taking summer courses. After my course work was completed, I prepared for the certification exam and passed. A year later, I began working on a new goal. I wanted to pursue my Masters degree in educational administration and become a certified school administrator. I still had the passion for teaching and helping students reach their goals, but I wanted to seek a different career path to promote student achievement. Thus, I set a goal to become a school principal. After I achieved this goal in three years while teaching full-time, I set yet another challenging goal. To quote Arnold H. Glasow, "Success isn't a result of spontaneous combustion. You must set yourself on fire." During this period in my life, I was on fire!

This time, I wanted to pursue a doctoral degree. The pursuit of this degree was driven by my desire to teach teachers how to become better teachers and address the needs of a diverse student population. I completed the doctoral program in half the time because I stopped working full-time to focus on my studies. During the first semester of working toward my doctoral degree, I got married. In the second year, while writing my dissertation proposal, I was accepted into an internship program at the Education Testing Service (ETS) in Princeton, New Jersey. I was achieving milestone after milestone. At the end of the spring semester the following year, I achieved one of the ultimate milestones in my life; I graduated with a Doctorate of Education degree in historical, social, and cultural foundation. Today, I am a college professor and my family and friends, including my parents, call me Doctor.

My story may be similar to what others have experienced in their educational journey. We all need to take ownership of our own goals and aspirations. The process of choosing the right career path led me to an important question: *What if I had lived my entire life in the wrong profession?* Thus, a few points are offered below:
- Guard your goals and aspirations with your heart. Your goals are just that, they are *your* goals.
- Be aware that some people may not understand your goals, aspirations, or dreams. It is okay that others do not "get" you and your dreams as these are personal endeavors that you have set out to accomplish.
- Set multiple short term and long term goals as you must constantly reassess where you are going and, ultimately, where you want to end up in your journey.
- Measure the success of achieving your goal by a barometer that is uniquely your own.

Professor Lisa A. Jones
University of Houston—Clear Lake

An Open Letter to College Students

Dear College Students,

Most of you are beginning your college education, whereas others are current students getting ready to exit the undergraduate phase of college to enter the "real world." From the first day you step on campus, you must enter those doors with an unrelenting sense of urgency to achieve academic success. College is a place for social and intellectual growth. During your stay, make sure to answer the all-important question, "Why am I going to college?" The answer should be to achieve academic success and prepare yourself for life after graduation.

Before I close this chapter of the book, I want you to envision yourself registering for the last semester of courses to complete your graduation requirements. Continue to maintain an exuberant approach to making the best grades possible. In that semester, you will apply for graduation. The university will send you a letter confirming that you have fulfilled the requirements as long as you uphold your current academic regiment. Then you'll be able to inform your family and friends of the graduation date by sending them formal invitations. Next, you'll get fitted for your cap and gown and receive it shortly after.

On graduation day, you'll enter a ballroom, gymnasium, or hall that will house all of the college graduates prior to the ceremony. For some students, this will be a defining moment when you reflect on your undergraduate career. There will be a mix of emotions, ranging from excitement to fear. You will be excited to graduate and fearful of the unknown after graduation. When you enter into the formation to the main area of the graduation ceremony, you'll observe a sea of people waiting to cheer you on. In that crowd will be family, friends, professors, and staff that are extremely proud of you for accomplishing this academic goal. The announcer will call your section by major, and you will stand and walk toward the stage. Afterward, they will call your name, and the crowd will erupt with joy and happiness. I want you to treasure this moment because you deserve it. Congratulations!

NAME _____   DATE _____

Questions for Personal Growth

1. Who are the individuals that have kept you motivated? Find three specific tangible things to focus on to keep you motivated.

2. Are you planning for the "real world"? What will you do after graduation? Have you chosen the correct career path?

3. Why does one person succeed whereas another fails? Have you resigned your life to mediocrity? Or, are you destined for greatness?

CHAPTER SIX
Living a Significant Life

"Living a Significant Life."
(Abbreviated Version)

To those whom much is given, much is expected / This philosophy transcends beyond success / And moves humanity forward / For the betterment of mankind and womankind

After obtaining success / We should all strive to become significant/ And roam the earth in a state of presence / Giving love and support to people / In the name of compassion / Remaking ourselves as both powerful communicators of love and lovers of all people

If we want ultimate happiness / Live a life of significance/ Give back/ Pay it forward / For good deeds bred love / And we were all born to spread love

Hoston (2016); *written after having my son, William T. Hoston Jr.*

Significant

JACKIE ROBINSON ONCE SAID, "A LIFE ISN'T SIGNIFICANT except for its impact on other lives." He is perhaps the most significant baseball player to ever live for breaking the color barrier in Major League Baseball (MLB). When Robinson broke into the major leagues on April 15, 1947, with the Brooklyn Dodgers, more than 60 years of racial segregation came to an end for black players in baseball. He officially became the first black player in MLB.

In addition to overcoming racial obstacles, he had an amazing baseball career in a short span with the Brooklyn Dodgers. During his ten-year MLB career, Robinson went on to win the Rookie of the Year (ROY) award in 1947, the Most Valuable Player (MVP) award in 1949 as the first black player honored, was an All-Star in six consecutive seasons (1949-1954), and helped the Dodgers to win the World Series championship in 1955. On January 5, 1957, at the age of 37, he retired from the game. Years later, in 1962, Robinson was inducted into the MLB Hall of Fame.

How Significant Is Your Life?

Success |noun| the achievement of one's goals.

Significant |adjective| to have an effect.

How significant is your life? There is a major difference between "achieving successful" and "living a significant life." *Success* implies that an individual has completed all (or most) of their life goals, whereas, *significance* identifies that intervals of success happen on the journey to fulfill God's ultimate purpose for our lives.

When a person is driven to become successful, they develop an insatiable appetite for success. It becomes a part of their being. In the words of writer and Civil Rights leader, Howard Thurman, "Deep is

After retiring from playing baseball, Robinson became an active member in the fight for equal rights and protections for black Americans. He was a champion for social and political causes. The Rev. Dr. Martin Luther King Jr. once called him "a legend and symbol in his own time" who "challenged the dark skies of intolerance and frustration."

Major League Baseball universally retired Robinson's uniform Number "42" in 1997. He was the first player ever to receive such an honor. Since 2009, each year on April 15, which is named "Jackie Robinson Day," MLB has adopted a tradition for all of its players and on-field personnel to wear Number 42 in honor of Robinson. While he was "successful" on the baseball field, today's players celebrate the "significance" of Robinson's life off of the field. Jackie Robinson lived a significant life.

the hunger." This means, having a deep hunger to achieve more in life. One of Thurman's most known quotes is, "Don't ask what the world needs. Ask what makes you come alive, and go do it. Because what the world needs is people who have come alive." Within the context of this quote, he is explaining how success manifests into significance.

Comparing our lives to that of Jackie Robinson is an immeasurable feat. Nonetheless, after a student graduates from college, gets a well-paying job, starts a family, and attains by their own definition the "American Dream"—all great accomplishments on the successful path to prosperity—he or she will at some point have to ask themselves: Is this it? Is this all life has to offer? These introspective questions should then make them say to themselves, "Success cannot be the end goal. While

I am appreciative for all of the things I have accomplished, there is more work to do in this lifetime."

Then another set of questions may emerge into their conscience: Why am I not satisfied? What continues to still be my motivation for pursuing success? Why am I still hungry to fulfill another component of life? What is my impact on the lives of others?

Listed below are three ways to make your life significant. Read these to shine a light on what it takes to live a life beyond the subjective notion of success.

1. Become a Mentor

Mentoring others is the Number One way to make your life significant. A mentor is someone who can provide advice and guidance to another person (i.e., mentee) to accomplish their goals. In this nurturing role, you take the valuable information you have learned and then pass along this knowledge to unselfishly help others. In the words of the renowned poet and Civil Rights activist, Maya Angelou, "When you learn, teach, when you get, give."

Successful mentors wholeheartedly embrace this role, and as well, hope for their mentees to accomplish their own goals. The passing along of knowledge is critical in the role of mentor because it creates a generative effect to understand that academic and career success can only be attained with help. When you realize this, it establishes a symbiotic desire, and you now believe it is your duty to help others. As a result, your life will begin to evolve from the societal constructed label of "successful" to the humanitarian label of "significant," which will lead to an immense feeling of self-worth and fulfillment.

2. Be Enthusiastic about Life

Be enthusiastic about life, and it will help you influence the lives of others. When you live a life built on the principles of morals, values, integrity, and goodwill, it will draw people to you like a magnet. As simple as it sounds, it is true. People want to encounter, interact, and spend time with those who are enthusiastic about life. Enthusiasm breeds enthusiasm.

How likable are you? Enthusiasm leads to likability. One of the ways to be significant is to be likable without compromising your self-worth. Will you encounter people who are jealous of your enthusiasm? Yes. However, you must continue to be optimistic, kind to others, a pillar of joy and love, and allow your magnetism to be a light of hope for others.

3. Practice Humility Regarding Success

Practicing humility regarding success is imperative. For example, appreciate your success, but don't use your success to inadvertently place negative energy into the universe. Sometimes people who have achieved academic and career success cross the thin line of humility. By no means should you keep your successes to yourself or minimize your achievements, however, don't get lulled by your ego into a mindset of intentionally or unintentionally *criticizing people* and *complaining about things* related to people who haven't achieved success at the same rate or level. Don't relegate their lack of success to merely "being lazy," "not committed," or "undisciplined." People who live a life of significance encourage through positive words and actions rather than discourage with words of failure and a body language of dissatisfaction.

Appreciate your success, but value the opportunity to be significant in the lives of others. There is no greater sense of self-worth and fulfillment than when attempting to lend a hand to uplift others. This is important because there are too many people in this world in need of help.

In conclusion, live a life of significance. Personally, my goal in life is to help as many current students and graduates as possible. Thus, I desire for my legacy to be invested in the act of service. This will define my significance. It is more important for me to be "significant" than "successful."

After a student achieves academic and career success, I love for them to contact me via email or friend me on social media for me to witness how their life has evolved. It gives me great pleasure to see some of the wonderful things that past students are doing to help others. Students who once entered my classroom at 18-years-old with no paper, pencil, or book, are now creating scholarships to send graduating high school students to college and mentoring the students throughout their college years. In the words of writer Charles Dickens, their evolution to a life of significance is proof that "No one is useless in this world who lightens the burdens of another." Live a life of significance!

NAME _____   DATE _____

Questions for Personal Growth

1. What does your ideal life look like beyond graduation?

2. In general, what has been your impact on the lives of others?

3. Write down and explain one thing you can do to make your life significant not mentioned in the chapter.

Exercise #2: Academic Preparation for the Semester.

Instructions: In college, students are expected to be independent learners. Students are expected to attend class, obtain study materials such as books, take good notes, and independently study all of the materials. The average student is expected to study 4-6 hours a day to achieve academic success. For one semester, write down your exam dates, study time per exam, and exam grades for each course.

Course #1	Exam Date	Study Time	Exam Grade
_____	_____	_____	_____
_____	_____	_____	_____
_____	_____	_____	_____
_____	_____	_____	_____

Course #2	Exam Date	Study Time	Exam Grade
_____	_____	_____	_____
_____	_____	_____	_____
_____	_____	_____	_____
_____	_____	_____	_____

Course #3	Exam Date	Study Time	Exam Grade
_____	_____	_____	_____
_____	_____	_____	_____
_____	_____	_____	_____
_____	_____	_____	_____

Course #4   Exam Date   Study Time   Exam Grade

_____   _____   _____   _____
_____   _____   _____   _____
_____   _____   _____   _____
_____   _____   _____   _____

Course #5   Exam Date   Study Time   Exam Grade

_____   _____   _____   _____
_____   _____   _____   _____
_____   _____   _____   _____
_____   _____   _____   _____

Course #6   Exam Date   Study Time   Exam Grade

_____   _____   _____   _____
_____   _____   _____   _____
_____   _____   _____   _____
_____   _____   _____   _____

Exercise #4: How to Avoid Procrastination, Part II.

Instructions: Track your academic productivity for an entire week. Do this preferably the week before midterm exams. Keep track of the completed tasks throughout the day to ensure that you are on pace to make the best possible grades for your exams. Write down the time and day of the completed task.

Time	Monday	Tuesday	Wednesday	Thursday	Friday	Saturday	Sunday
7:00 a.m.							
8:00 a.m.							
9:00 a.m.							
10:00 a.m.							
11:00 a.m.							
12:00 p.m.							
1:00 p.m.							
2:00 p.m.							
3:00 p.m.							
4:00 p.m.							
5:00 p.m.							
6:00 p.m.							
7:00 p.m.							
8:00 p.m.							
9:00 p.m.							
10:00 p.m.							
11:00 p.m.							
12:00 a.m.							

Exercise #5: Ways to Maintain a High G.P.A.

Instructions: Grade Point Average, or G.P.A., represents the average of a student's course grades. It is important for students to maintain a relatively high G.P.A. in college for future success. In Part I, check the boxes that apply. Each checked box is viewed as a contributing factor to maintain a relatively high G.P.A. Be as honest with yourself as possible. In Part II, choose three of the boxes not checked. Write down how to improve in these areas.

Part I:

1. Go to Class Regularly ❏
2. Sit in the Front ❏
3. Participate in Class Discussion ❏
4. Take Notes in Class ❏
5. Read the Class Materials ❏
6. Joined or Formed a Study Group ❏
7. Studied 4-6 Hours a Day ❏
8. Created a Date and Time Calendar ❏
9. Talked to Your Professor ❏
10. Met with Academic Advisor ❏
11. Met with Peer Mentor ❏
12. Obtained a Tutor with TutorTrac ❏
13. Attended Academic Skills Workshops ❏
14. Acquired Information about Library Services ❏
15. Used Rewards as Incentive ❏

Part II:

_____

_____

_____

_____

Exercise #6: Preparing for an Examination Checklist.

Instructions: Answer the questions below.

1. Course Name and Number: _____
2. Date and Time of Exam: _____
3. Date Began Studying: _____
4. Date Ended Studying: _____
5. List All of the Readings for the Exam: a. _____

   b. _____

   c. _____

   d. _____
6. Have the Exam Review? (Yes/No): _____
7. If 'No' to #6, Made Exam Review? (Yes/No):
   _____
8. Familiar with Exam Topics? (Yes/No):
   _____
9. Need Clarification from Professor? (Yes/No):
   _____
10. If 'Yes' to #8, Contacted Professor? (Yes/No):
    _____

Exercise #9: Check Your Positive Attitude.

Instructions: In Part I, for each of the following statements, rate yourself on a scale from 1 to 10 (with 10 being the highest). In Part II, identify the answer choices of 6 and below and write down how to personally address these areas.

Part I:

I like the person who I am today.

1 2 3 4 5 6 7 8 9 10

I know precisely what I want in life.

1 2 3 4 5 6 7 8 9 10

I know what is holding me back from achieving my goals.

1 2 3 4 5 6 7 8 9 10

If I had to be who I am today for the rest of my life, I would be happy.

1 2 3 4 5 6 7 8 9 10

I am proud of myself.

1 2 3 4 5 6 7 8 9 10

Part II:

_____
_____
_____
_____
_____
_____

Exercise #11: The 'Goal' Grid.

Instructions: Fill in the 'Goal' Grid below.

A. *The Goal*: What do you want to achieve?	B. *The Plan*: What plans or actions to achieve the goal?
C. *The Obstacles*: What obstacles might you face in pursuit of the goal?	D. *The Outcome*: Did you achieve the goal? Are you satisfied with the accomplishment?

Exercise #12: 'The Story of the Builder'.

Instructions: Read the following story. As you consider 'The Story of the Builder,' answer the question afterwards.

An elderly man was ready to retire from a home building company. He told his supervisor that he appreciated the opportunity to work for the company for nearly 30 years, however, it was time to retire and enjoy his family. The elderly man had been married for 26 years. He and his wife had five children and twelve grandchildren. This was the perfect time to retire.

His supervisor was considerate of the decision to retire, but requested that the elderly man build one last home. Since the elderly man was such a hard worker, the supervisor asked if he could build this last home as a personal favor. The elderly man said, "Yes." The supervisor recommended that the elderly man use the best materials for the home. For this home, he was to use a brick and marble exterior, build four bedrooms, a huge master bedroom, entertainment room, dining room, work office, swimming pool, add hardwood floors, granite countertops, marble sinks, garden tubs, etc. Instead of adhering to the supervisor's requests, the elderly man used substandard materials, resorted to poor workmanship, and made a few costly errors in judgment building the foundation of the home. He worked just hard enough to complete the home. The supervisor asked him to build an extraordinary home, but the elderly man built an ordinary home.

When the elderly man was finished with the home, the supervisor came to inspect his work. Although disappointed that the elderly man did not adhere to his recommendations, the supervisor handed him the keys to the home and said, "This is your new home. My retirement present to you."

The elderly man was stunned! The look of disappointment illuminated on his face. If he had known that the home he was building would be his own, maybe he would have listened to his supervisor and built a luxurious home. It would have been an awesome gift for all of his hard work over the years.

(Adaptation–Hoston version)

Exercise #14: What Is Your G.P.A.?

Instructions: Write down your G.reatest P.ersonal A.chievement to date.

About the Author

DR. WILLIAM T. HOSTON Sr., Ph.D., is a professor, author, motivational speaker, poet, and documentarian who hails from New Orleans, Louisiana. He is associate professor of political science at the University of Houston – Clear Lake (UHCL). Dr. Hoston holds research interests in the areas of minority voting behavior, political behavior of Black politicians, race and minority group behavior, Black masculinity, sexualities and gender, race and crime, and theories and dynamics of racism and oppression. His work traverses multiple genres, including editorials, essays, fiction, and poetry.

Dr. Hoston is the author or editor of 15 books; most recently, *Power to the People: Ascending Beyond Racism* (2018), *New Perspectives on Race and Ethnicity* (2018), *The Magic Beard* (2017), *I Love You, Son* (2017), *Race and the Black Male Subculture: The Lives of Toby Waller* (2016), *RNIT* (2016, 2015), and *Black Masculinity in the Obama Era: Outliers of Society* (2014). He is currently completing two academic books: *Toxic Silence: Race, Black Gender Identity, and Addressing the Violence against Black Transgender Women in Houston, TX*, and *Acts of Mobilization and Activism: A Case Study Analysis of Modern-Day College Protests*.

Dr. Hoston has proven his dedication and commitment to empowering youth and college students to have a brighter future, which was recognized by UHCL as he was the recipient of the 2013 Minnie Stevens Piper Award for outstanding teaching. He also was ranked in the 2012 - 2013 academic year as the 19th best college professor in America according to RateMyProfessor.com. Dr. Hoston's motto is, "I just want to be an example. Many have come before me, and hopefully, those that come after will be inspired by the example that I have set."

For more information on Dr. Hoston, please visit: WilliamHoston.com.

I Love You, Son

I tell my son, "I love you" all day, every day / For him to know that Daddy's love for him is infinite / Ever since he emerged from the womb / And placed a never-ending smile on my face / My life has not been the same / The ghosts who haunted my past / Have befriended me / Casper is no longer my enemy

I hug and kiss my son all day, every day / For him to know what Daddy's physical love feels like / Endless forms of Black male affection / To create a loving Black male / And eradicate Black masculine stereotypes

He won't be too tough to hug Daddy / He won't be too tough to kiss Daddy / Our love for each other will be expressive / I want him to be a bundle of joy

There will be times / That I cry when I see my son / He will ask, "Daddy, why are you crying?" / My reply will be, "Because I love you, son."

~*Hoston (2017)*

A Novelty: Mildred H. Hoston

Dear William Jr.,

Let me present to you a short novel about a novelty: Your great-grandmother, Mildred H. Hoston. She was the daughter of the late Milton Hooks and Artist Battle-Hooks and wife of the Reverend Reed Hoston Jr.

I'm reminiscing about a place called home. It was on Route 1 in the red dirt plains of Leslie, Georgia. I cannot tell you how to get there, but I can show you how to get there. The heart has its own compass. Leslie, Georgia is a tiny dot on the map known for rolling farmland and rumbling tractors. Incorporated in 1892, the town has a population of just over 400 people. It's the kind of town that folks in big cities stop in only to pump gas. They pump, use the restroom, and then leave. However, Leslie, Georgia is so much more than farmland and tractors. It is so much more than a rest stop. This diacritical mark on the map once housed in life, and now in death, your great-grandmother.

I remember along the travel to see your great-grandmother was a long stretch of highway. Riding along this stretch, you could begin to feel the love permeating. Your great-grandmother's love filled the universe. The universe is an abundant place, however, her love could occupy spaces unknown to the seeing-eye. Her love spoke into you. Her love was the reason we believe in the goodness of people. If one paid attention to every detail of how she loved, such a lesson could change the world. She was a school teacher for 35 years, but she was a life teacher and lover of people all of her life. God put His hands on her and never took them off.

Before reaching the entrance to her house, there was a narrow gravel road that led to the final destination. There was no doorbell on the house. The crackling of the rocks from the gravel road would alert her to your presence. Down the hill, you went. She would eventually appear on the porch. Once you got out of the car, she was always there waiting with open arms. "That's my sweet boy," your great-grandmother would say, echoing her joy to see me to your great-grandfather. From her, I inherited a sense of self-confidence. She was a builder of people—hugs, kisses, and words of affirmation were her tools.

"Hug grandma," she would say with a joyous smile. Once she saw you, you knew a big hug would be waiting. She would give a hug big enough to smother a grizzly bear. You knew a big kiss would be waiting. She would deliver a big kiss on your cheek that smelled like BBQ ribs, collard greens, mac and cheese, and sweet yams—my favorite meal. "Let grandma see you," she would say.

She never asked, "How much food do you want on your plate?" It was a plate full of food, and she expected you to eat it all.

For dessert, she would serve a homemade blackberry pie with homemade vanilla ice cream. She would always top it with fresh blackberries. In the summer months, the blackberries grew on the trees along the gravel entrance. When I visited during the summer, I would spend many mornings, afternoons, and evenings picking and eating blackberries until my fingers were stained and my belly full of the ripe fruit.

After I licked both plates, she would ask, "Did you have enough, baby?"

"Yes ma'am," I replied. Then we would sit at the table and just talk.

Son, your great-grandmother could ask you about your bad day, and then put her finger under your chin and lift your head up and give you a speech about how tomorrow could possibly be the best day of your entire life. Her message was always: *God is life. Love cures all.* And equally important, she preached: *Be good to people. Find the good people. Be good people.*

I miss her. On my knees, I tell her about you. Like when your mother gave birth. Like when I first held you. Like when you first flipped over on your stomach. Like when you first said, "Daddy." Like when you took your first steps. Like when you kissed Ella. I tell her how you are inquisitive like your Uncle Feddrick and talk all day like your Aunt Jelena. Then I cry for her because she always said good memories should be followed by a good cry. I'm smiling while writing this. I'm crying while writing this. Because I know that meeting you, would have brought even more joy to her life.

~Hoston (2017)

February 11, 1974 – R.est I.n P.eace

I've lived from February 11, 1974 to the dash / I live in the dash / God asked me to punctuate my future / Therefore, I drew a line in the universe / To validate my existence / Flat line to the present / That was the only way to rise above the depths of my circumstances / I had a dark past / But now I have a bright future / A shining example of 'why' you should never give up

I walk with my head held high / Because I can't see Heaven looking down / I continue to smile to show life it hasn't disappointed me / Life is a gift, so I opened it / And it presented to me the ability to profess my love by helping others / According to Pablo Picasso / "The meaning of life is to find your gift / The purpose of life is to give it away" / Millions didn't make it / But I was one of the ones who did / Thus, I owe it to them / To give the voiceless, a voice / Those going nowhere, a road to travel / Those afraid to reach beyond themselves, a ladder to climb / And those that need to start over, a new beginning

I live in the dash / A place past my fears / My Ph.D. came from being P.oor, H.ungry, and D.etermined / I continue to take calculated risks / To prevent my dreams from dying / So one day, I can happily R.est I.n P.eace with no regrets

~Hoston (2013)

Index

absentee fathers, 26–27, 29, 31
academic advisors, 20, 46, 53–54, 56, 70, 98
academic greatness, 5, 63
academic success
    and attitude, 2–3
    and class attendance, 50, 51, 68
    and class participation, 50, 68, 69, 70
    and failing moments, 16–19, 106
    and good manners, 50–51
    and helping others, 96–97
    and imagination, 5
    individual definitions of, 6
    nontraditional approach to, 82
    and self-triumph, 5
    sense of urgency, 103
    strategies for, 51–52, 70
    and work ethic, 63
accountability, 100
Acheson, Dean, 99
active listening, 68, 100
advisor meetings, 53–54, 56
Ali, Muhammad, 16–17
"American Dream," 109
Anderson, Shaun M., 81–83
"And I Made Lemonade" (Hoston), 1
Angelou, Maya, 11, 110
Apollinaire, Guillaume, 97
Arkansas State University, 82
attitude
    academic challenges, 7
    in academic success, 2–3
    and failure, 4–5

    importance of, 2
    toward learning, 68
    and motivation, 4
    negative, 2–3, 4, 5, 70
    and personal hurdles, 3
    positive, 2, 3, 4, 5, 7, 10, 16, 17, 68, 70
    responsibility for, 2
    and self-esteem, 7–9
    and self-healing, 6–7
    and self-motivation, 9–11
    and self-triumph, 5–6, 24
    and T.H.E.M., 4–5

Bannister-Yarde, Jennifer Alexandria, 79–81
Bannister-Yarde, Jonathan Campbell, 81
"Black Tax" (Hoston), 43
Bolling, William, 52
Boys and Girls Clubs of America, 59
Burnett, Angela, 80
Butler, Mrs., 47–49, 51
Butterworth, Eric, 90

Campbell, Joseph, 26
Cankeyo: You Can Keep Your Dreams Alive (Gray), 11
career aspirations, 101–103
Churchill, Winston, 77
Clark, Eugene B., 29
Clark, Frank A., 79
Clark, Shanquilla, 29
class attendance, 50, 51, 68
class participation, 50, 68, 69, 70

Clements-Martin, Rolonda, 38
college education
    and advanced degrees, 6
    first-year transitions, 7–8
    majors, 6
    need for, 59
    value of, 5, 69, 81
Confucius, 6
constructive criticism, 5
Cosby, Elgin, 38
courage
    and abuse, 83–84
    belief in students, 66–67, 76–77
    and death in family, 78–79, 81
    and failure, 68
    and health issues, 67
    and illness, 79–81
    and incarceration, 85–86
    lack of, 68
    and mentoring, 66–67, 76–77, 86–87
    and parental abandonment, 84–85
    and persistence, 78
    and personal growth, 89–90, 94
    and poverty, 81–82
    and truth, 101
Couser, Wendy L., 83–87
Cuban Four, 74–77

Dafoe, Willem, 47
D'Angelo, Anthony, 7
decision making, 99
"Deep is the Hunger," 108–109
determination, 44, 45–46, 47, 59, 61, 83
Devlin, Bernadette, 92
Dorris, Ronald, 60, 61
Douglass, Frederick, 29
Duffey, Jeffery "Fly," 9, 28
Duplessis, Pat, 45–47

Einstein, Albert, 5
Eliot, George, 8
Emerson, Ralph Waldo, 7, 66
enthusiastic about life, 110–111

Facebook, 51
faith, 26, 27, 28, 83, 86–87
fearlessness, 82–83

first-year students
    and academic advisors, 70
    checklist, 20–21
    desire for advanced degrees, 9–10
    growth of, 97
    transition to college, 7–8, 68
    work ethic of, 59
Florida A&M University (FAMU), 57
Florida State University
    and Cuban Four, 74–77
    and racial discrimination, 1, 54–58
    and teaching, 17, 38
Forbes, Malcolm, 49

Gandhi, Mahatma, 96
GED (General Educational Development test), 36, 37
Gifford, Dr., 53–54, 55
Glasow, Arnold H., 46, 99, 102
The Godfather (1972), 71
grades
    achievement of, 53, 70, 103
    complacency toward, 70, 75
    focus on, 4–5, 48, 55, 70
    improvement of, 46–47, 48, 58–59
    lack of, 49
    and plagiarism, 71
    and professors, 15
    and self-esteem, 8
    and work ethic, 58
graduation
    and career success, 98–100, 104
    ceremony, 94, 96–97, 104
    from high school, 28, 85
    from Masters program, 1, 37
    from Ph.D. program, 35, 37, 61
    and post-graduation check list, 98
    preparation for, 97, 104
Gray, LaKeisha, 9–11
    Cankeyo: You Can Keep Your Dreams Alive, 11
GRE (graduate record examination), 54, 75

Harbaugh, Jack, 44–45
Harbaugh, Jim, 44

Harbaugh, John, 44
Hoston, Cleveland
   and absentee father, 27, 29, 31
   and childhood circumstances, 28–29
   criminal activity, 30, 31
Hoston, Feddrick
   and absentee father, 29, 31
   and childhood circumstances, 28–29
   criminal activity, 29–30, 31
   incarceration of, 1, 30, 31
Hoston, Mildred, 1, 7, 27, 28, 29, 32, 34, 37, 92–94, 96
Hoston, Reed, 27
Hoston, William (Love)
   as absentee father, 26–27, 29, 31
   adoption of, 93
Hoston, William T.
   and absentee father, 26–27, 31
   academic grades, 43, 45–47, 48, 53, 55, 60, 61
   affirmation from family and friends, 37–38
   birth of, 33
   and childhood job, 32–33
   and dysfunctional family, 26
   education
      earns Masters degree, 55, 74, 93
      Florida State University, 1, 38, 43, 54–58, 59, 65, 77, 92, 94
      and graduations, 28, 35, 37
      Nicholls State University, 45, 48
      Oxnard Community College, 47–49, 53
      and Ph.D. comprehensive exams, 55–56, 57, 77
      and Ph.D. program, 55, 58, 59, 60–61, 65, 77, 94
   financial support for mother, 32–33
   and helping others, 96–97
   mentorship of, 86–87
   on mindfulness, 99
   participation in sports, 28, 45, 46
   racial discrimination of, 1, 54–58
   relationship with brothers, 26, 29–31
   relationship with mother, 26, 33–35, 38, 96
   support of students, 76–77

teaching
   evaluations, 18
   Florida State University, 17, 74
   philosophy of, 17–19, 66, 74
   UHCL, 66
   Wichita State University, 61
   Xavier University, 59–60
   University of New Orleans, 20, 51–54, 59, 60
humility, 15–16, 94
   practicing, regarding success, 111–112
Hurricane Katrina, 25, 60–61

Instagram, 51

Jamison, Josh, 54
Jones, Lisa A., 101–103

King, Jr., Martin Luther, 61
Korda, Michael, 100

Lasorda, Tommy, 61
LGBTQ students, 73
Lincoln, Abraham, 33
"Living a Significant Life" (Hoston), 107
Lombardi, Vince, 5–6
LSAT
   exam, 4, 66, 75, 95
   preparation, 3, 66, 76

Man and Superman: a Comedy and Philosophy (Shaw), 97
manners, 50–51
MCAT (Medical College Admission Test), 101
mediocrity, 5, 9, 13, 95, 106
mentor, 110
mentoring, 110
Miami Dade Community College (MDC), 74
Miami University (Ohio), 44
mindfulness, 98–99
Mitchell, Bertha Mae, 33, 96
motivation
   ability to maintain, 4, 105
   and attitude, 4
   death in family, 78–79

motivation (*Continued*)
    and friendship, 75–76
    and quality of life, 35–37
    questionnaire, 13, 15
    and self-talk, 58–59
    and testimony, 89
motivational worksheets, 115–143

National Collegiate Athletic Association (NCAA), 45
NCAA (National Collegiate Athletic Association), 45
negative attitude, 2–3, 4, 5, 70
networking, 99
Nicholls State University (NSU), 20, 45, 46–47
nontraditional students, 8–9
North Carolina State University (NCSU), 36
Northwestern State University (NSU), 9, 45

Oliver, Mary, 35
"Our Deepest Fears" (Williamson), 92
Owens, Thelma C., 96
Oxnard Community College (OCC), 47–49, 53

Pacino, Al, 71
"Pain" (Hoston), 25
Parsons, Keith M., 51, 72
perseverance, 92–93, 94–96
personal growth
    and academic greatness, 63
    and achieving goals, 23, 63
    and courage, 89–90
    and happiness, 23
    motivation, 105
    and pride in self, 41–42
    and self-triumph, 24
Piedra, Joel "Joey," 74, 75, 76–77
plagiarism, 70–72
Plato, 26–27
positive attitude, 2, 3, 4, 5, 7, 10, 16, 17, 68, 70
post-graduation
    and career plans, 105
    checklist, 98

poverty, 81–82
practicing humility
    regarding success, 111–112
pride in self, 37–39, 41–42
professors
    communication with, 49–50
    interaction with, 15–16, 68, 69
The Pursuit of Happyness (2006), 94

quality of life, 35–37, 67, 98

racial discrimination
    at Florida State University, 1, 54–58
    limited support from faculty and administration, 56–57
Radmacher, Mary Anne, 78
Robinson, Jackie, 108

Schuller, Robert H., 6
self-belief, 100
self-esteem, 7–9
self-healing, 6–7
self-motivation, 9–11
self-triumph, 5–6, 24
Shakespeare, William, 3
Shaw, George Bernard, 97
significant, 108–109
Simon, Shaun R., 73
Smith, Janet
    and alcohol abuse, 33–35
    background, 33
    joins Navy, 33
    relationship with son, 47, 96
    work ethic of, 32
Smith, Will, 94
Snapchat, 51
Southern University Law Center (SULC), 10
St. Thomas University, 75
Stetson University, 75
students
    first-year, 8, 9, 20–21, 59, 68, 70, 97
    LGBTQ, 73
    nontraditional, 8–9
    groups, 8, 68
    support of, 76–77
    transfer, 20–21
study environment, 51

study groups, 52
study habits, 51, 68
study schedule, 52–53
success, practicing humility regarding, 111–112

"The End Result" (Hoston), 91
"The Window of Opportunity" (Hoston), 65
Thurman, Howard, 108
time management, 52
transfer students, 20–21
Tubman, Harriet, 93
Twitter, 51

University of Arkansas, 82
University of Houston—Clear Lake (UHCL), 3, 4, 51, 66, 72, 73, 80, 95, 103

University of Michigan, 44
University of New Orleans (UNO), 20, 51–54, 59, 60
Uses of Sorrow (Oliver), 35

Vance, Kim, 38

West Virginia University, 82
Wichita State University (WSU), 8, 57, 58, 61, 86
Wike, Angelina, 78–79
Williamson, Marianne, 92

Xavier University, 7, 59–60

Yeager, Dexter, 100
YouTube, 51

CPSIA information can be obtained
at www.ICGtesting.com
Printed in the USA
LVHW021654081218
599715LV00007B/17/P